America's Urban-Rural Divide

Bridey Heing, Book Editor

GREENHAVEN
PUBLISHING

Published in 2020 by Greenhaven Publishing, LLC
353 3rd Avenue, Suite 255, New York, NY 10010

Copyright © 2020 by Greenhaven Publishing, LLC

First Edition

Articles in Greenhaven Publishing anthologies are often edited for length to meet page requirements. In addition, original titles of these works are changed to clearly present the main thesis and to explicitly indicate the author's opinion. Every effort is made to ensure that Greenhaven Publishing accurately reflects the original intent of the authors. Every effort has been made to trace the owners of the copyrighted material.

Library of Congress Cataloging-in-Publication Data

Names: Heing, Bridey, editor.
Title: America's urban-rural divide / Bridey Heing, book editor.
Description: First edition. | New York : Greenhaven Publishing, 2020. | Series: Introducing issues with opposing viewpoints | Includes bibliographical references and index. | Audience: Grades 7–12.
Identifiers: LCCN 2019022851 | ISBN 9781534506619 (library binding) | ISBN 9781534506602 (paperback)
Subjects: LCSH: Rural-urban relations—United States—History—Juvenile literature. | Group values (Sociology)—United States—Juvenile literature. | Democracy—United States—Juvenile literature. | United States—Politics and government—2017—Juvenile literature.
Classification: LCC HT384.U5 A58 2020 | DDC 307.70973—dc23
LC record available at https://lccn.loc.gov/2019022851

Manufactured in the United States of America

Website: http://greenhavenpublishing.com

Contents

Chapter 3: How Can the Urban-Rural Divide Be Addressed?

Foreword

Indulging in a wide spectrum of ideas, beliefs, and perspectives is a critical cornerstone of democracy. After all, it is often debates over differences of opinion, such as whether to legalize abortion, how to treat prisoners, or when to enact the death penalty, that shape our society and drive it forward. Such diversity of thought is frequently regarded as the hallmark of a healthy and civilized culture. As the Reverend Clifford Schutjer of the First Congregational Church in Mansfield, Ohio, declared in a 2001 sermon, "Surrounding oneself with only like-minded people, restricting what we listen to or read only to what we find agreeable is irresponsible. Refusing to entertain doubts once we make up our minds is a subtle but deadly form of arrogance." With this advice in mind, Introducing Issues with Opposing Viewpoints books aim to open readers' minds to the critically divergent views that comprise our world's most important debates.

Introducing Issues with Opposing Viewpoints simplifies for students the enormous and often overwhelming mass of material now available via print and electronic media. Collected in every volume is an array of opinions that captures the essence of a particular controversy or topic. Introducing Issues with Opposing Viewpoints books embody the spirit of nineteenth-century journalist Charles A. Dana's axiom: "Fight for your opinions, but do not believe that they contain the whole truth, or the only truth." Absorbing such contrasting opinions teaches students to analyze the strength of an argument and compare it to its opposition. From this process readers can inform and strengthen their own opinions, or be exposed to new information that will change their minds. Introducing Issues with Opposing Viewpoints is a mosaic of different voices. The authors are statesmen, pundits, academics, journalists, corporations, and ordinary people who have felt compelled to share their experiences and ideas in a public forum. Their words have been collected from newspapers, journals, books, speeches, interviews, and the Internet, the fastest growing body of opinionated material in the world.

Introducing Issues with Opposing Viewpoints shares many of the well-known features of its critically acclaimed parent series, Opposing

Viewpoints. The articles allow readers to absorb and compare divergent perspectives. Active reading questions preface each viewpoint, requiring the student to approach the material thoughtfully and carefully. Photographs, charts, and graphs supplement each article. A thorough introduction provides readers with crucial background on an issue. An annotated bibliography points the reader toward articles, books, and websites that contain additional information on the topic. An appendix of organizations to contact contains a wide variety of charities, nonprofit organizations, political groups, and private enterprises that each hold a position on the issue at hand. Finally, a comprehensive index allows readers to locate content quickly and efficiently.

Introducing Issues with Opposing Viewpoints is also significantly different from Opposing Viewpoints. As the series title implies, its presentation will help introduce students to the concept of opposing viewpoints and learn to use this material to aid in critical writing and debate. The series' four-color, accessible format makes the books attractive and inviting to readers of all levels. In addition, each viewpoint has been carefully edited to maximize a reader's understanding of the content. Short but thorough viewpoints capture the essence of an argument. A substantial, thought-provoking essay question placed at the end of each viewpoint asks the student to further investigate the issues raised in the viewpoint, compare and contrast two authors' arguments, or consider how one might go about forming an opinion on the topic at hand. Each viewpoint contains sidebars that include at-a-glance information and handy statistics. A Facts About section located in the back of the book further supplies students with relevant facts and figures.

Following in the tradition of the Opposing Viewpoints series, Greenhaven Publishing continues to provide readers with invaluable exposure to the controversial issues that shape our world. As John Stuart Mill once wrote: "The only way in which a human being can make some approach to knowing the whole of a subject is by hearing what can be said about it by persons of every variety of opinion and studying all modes in which it can be looked at by every character of mind. No wise man ever acquired his wisdom in any mode but this." It is to this principle that Introducing Issues with Opposing Viewpoints books are dedicated.

Introduction

"Inequality is not just an issue between individuals, between classes, between regions. It's between urban and rural."
        —*Michael Ignatieff, Canadian author, academic, and former politician*

When we think about opposites, it is likely that urban and rural come to mind fairly quickly. We are all taught that cities—or urban spaces—are fundamentally different from the country—or rural spaces, like farmland and homes located outside of towns. These differences can be seen in population, transit, economy, noise level, and the way these places look. The hustle and bustle of the city is the polar opposite of the quiet and calm of the country.

But in recent years, those differences have come to be seen as a threat to the health of our democracy and the future of the United States. In addition to visible differences, many worry that differences between urban and rural residents point to two different visions for our country—and that the gap between the two might not be possible to bridge. While urban populations are seen as more liberal and diverse, rural populations are seen as more conservative and homogenous. Experts and observers alike fear that this divide is rooted in such deeply held values that the future of the country depends on overcoming differences to find a middle ground, but they are unsure how to do so.

The data supports this concern, as shown in research by the Pew Research Center and Michael Carolan included in this collection. Urban populations are more likely to support liberal policies, including immigration reform measures that ease restrictions, programs that increase government spending on non-defense-related work, and universal health care. Meanwhile, rural populations support conservative policies, such as immigration policies that restrict people coming to the US, privatization of services, and lower government spending. People living in both places also have distinct ideas about those living in the other setting: both urban and rural residents might argue that their counterparts are isolated in an echo chamber and unaware of the impact policies they support have outside of their own experience. Too often, these debates fall into a blame game with those on both sides of the divide arguing that the other is responsible for finding a solution.

But as some point out, trends aren't everything. Some feel the divide between urban and rural populations is not as dire as statistics suggest. They point out that people from across the political spectrum live all across the country—in cities and on farms alike. As the census data and Robin Warshaw's research in this anthology note, rural communities face the same issues as urban communities and are diverse in unique ways. Thinkers also argue that fundamental American values are almost universal and that this can help transcend differences at a time when polarization seems so heightened. In this collection, Christiana K. McFarland argues that the economic future of the country depends on the relationship between urban and rural communities.

Urban and rural populations are deeply connected, but in ways that aren't always clear. Historically, the United States was a rural and agricultural country, with most people living outside of urban centers. That began to change with industrialization and the rise of specialized work, which created economic opportunities for workers in cities. People began leaving rural areas in search of work and more opportunities, which has made cities the economic hubs they are today. The economic differences between urban and rural spaces has led to a few problems, including a smaller and smaller rural population and the sense among some that cities are prioritized over rural communities when it comes to tax spending. This concern doesn't always prove true; in some states, like Illinois, rural populations receive more in state spending than the Chicago metropolitan area, which receives just eighty cents of state spending for every dollar they pay in taxes, according to the Paul Simon Public Policy Institute at Southern Illinois University.

Whether real or imagined, the urban-rural divide has fostered a sense of division that experts worry will do lasting damage to American democracy. It is rooted in misunderstanding, worry for the future, a history of competition, differences in resources, and other issues that speak to larger, very real problems facing the United States. Suggestions for how to fix what many believe is broken range from encouraging travel outside of familiar places, to changing the way media covers rural areas, to doing a better job making sure the changes brought by technology benefit everyone equally.

The viewpoints in *Introducing Issues with Opposing Viewpoints: America's Urban-Rural Divide* offer a comprehensive idea of what the urban-rural divide looks like and feels like, as well as the impact it is having on the country. This volume explores the urban-rural divide from all sides, looking at the history of migration in the United States, the data that speaks to how this divide manifests, the way people on both sides of the issue see one another, and ultimately the ways in which experts think we can come together.

Chapter 1

How Has the Urban-Rural Divide Developed?

Though urban and rural areas can seem worlds away, these communities often come into close contact as urban areas continue to grow.

The Urban-Rural Divide Can Be Traced Back to Earlier US History

Eliza Griswold

"The history of this early east v west tension is essential reading for those who want to understand the roots of the anti-government and anti-elite attitudes held by many rural Americans."

The Civil War was the culmination of many divisions in the United States, including ideological, geographic, and economic differences. But while the conflict between the Union in the North and the Confederacy in the South is often thought of as being a fight between two distinct sides, Griswold argues that divisions existed even among the forces on the frontlines. Looking at western Pennsylvania, Griswold highlights the ways that rural and urban differences have created conflict for generations, shaping the current outlooks that seem to pit one against the other. Eliza Griswold is a journalist and the author of *The Tenth Parallel: Dispatches from the Faultline Between Christianity and Islam.*

AS YOU READ, CONSIDER THE FOLLOWING QUESTIONS:

1. The Whiskey Rebellion was caused by tension between which two groups?
2. What nationalities were the early settlers in western Pennsylvania?
3. What made the alliance between soldiers in the Civil War so fragile?

"The historical roots of the US rural-urban divide run deep," by Eliza Griswold, Guardian News and Media Limited, July 4, 2018. Reprinted by permission.

Over the fireplace at Mingo Creek Craft Distillers, a whiskey purveyor in the small town of Washington, Pennsylvania, a portrait of Alexander Hamilton hangs upside down. With snowy hair and a black velvet jacket, Hamilton wears an impassive look that might be described as hauteur. In 1791, to pay off debts the newly formed United States incurred during the revolutionary war, Hamilton imposed the first federal tax on the people of the region. By taxing their most lucrative product, whiskey, he became what he is here today: a villain representing the excesses of the federal government.

The town of Washington is only a six-hour drive from Manhattan, but it's a world away from the Broadway stage where Hamilton, clad in snug white knickers, enjoys a better reputation. The difference in regard between the two Hamiltons is a stark illustration of the mutual disdain between rural and urban Americans.

I noticed the upside-down portrait of Hamilton several years ago while in western Pennsylvania reporting for what would become *Amity and Prosperity: One Family and the Fracturing of America,* my book exploring the ways rural Americans have been left behind, and how their disenfranchisement has spawned cultural resentment against liberal, urban Americans.

I didn't understand the nature of that rage until I arrived in Amity, Pennsylvania. I was raised in the eastern part of the state—or commonwealth, as Pennsylvanians prefer to call it. Until my grandmother died, my family had lived on the same land since before the revolutionary war, and my ancestors billeted George Washington's soldiers at a place called Camp Woods in 1777. Nearly a century later, when the civil war began, my great-great-great grandfather, Gen George Gordon Meade, a well-educated Philadelphian who attended West Point, led the union army at the Battle of Gettysburg, a town lying between the eastern, more urban part of Pennsylvania and the rural west. That battle, which took place 155 years ago this week, helped decide the war's outcome, at enormous human cost. Gettysburg was the bloodiest battle ever fought on US soil; of the 160,000 men and boys who fought there, 51,000 were left wounded, missing or dead.

With this storied history running through my blood, I'd assumed that the common bond of being fellow Pennsylvanians would endear

As of 2019, Chicago is the third most populous city in the United States. It is often regarded as distinct from the more rural communities that dominate the rest of Illinois.

me to my western brethren and establish an easy rapport for me, despite being an outsider and a reporter. I was soon disabused of that notion. When I first showed up in Amity and visited a cattle farmer, he asked me, "Where are you from?"

"I live in New York City, but I'm from Philadelphia," I told him.

"That's two strikes against you," he replied.

On another occasion, I carried my own organic instant coffee into the local diner, Popcorn Willie, and asked for hot water. I had some organic sprouted wheat bread with me which I wondered if the waitress might toast, too, I said. Although she grudgingly complied, the looks I received, and deserved, revealed palpable disgust at my outsider ways—elite predilections that people in Amity and the nearby town of Prosperity had neither the time nor the means to indulge.

I would soon come to understand that the antipathies toward city dwellers in rural Pennsylvania have deep roots. They are part of a long, fraught history of tension between the elitism of eastern Pennsylvania and the populism of the west, which dates back to the early 1700s. As I researched this centuries-long enmity—one compounded by economic and social disenfranchisement born of coal, oil and gas production, and failed industrialization—I started to understand why rural Americans had such contempt for the urban elite: for centuries city-dwellers have relied on their country neighbors to supply the materials for urban growth, while ignoring the costs harvesting such materials entailed.

In Washington, Pennsylvania, which voted for Donald Trump by a margin of three to two, our current president is often described as a brick rural Americans launched through the window of urban, elite America. Although that analogy is in some ways true, the deepest roots of these frustrations aren't always understood. Since I began my reporting in Amity and Prosperity seven years ago, I came to grasp how these patterns and attitudes were unfolding long before the president's grandfather, the German immigrant Frederick Trump, arrived in America.

When rural Pennsylvanians launched the Whiskey Rebellion they were merely bringing to a head longstanding tensions between Philadelphia's cosmopolitan landed Quakers and the rural settlers along the state's western frontier.

The settlers were mostly landless Scots-Irish who'd arrived in the colonies fleeing poverty and religious persecution. They pushed west to squat on land that belonged to Native Americans, carving their initials in trees to claim forested plots by so-called "tomahawk rights."

These "back-inhabitants," as the Philadelphia gentry derisively called them, waged bloody battles with the native peoples over land. During the revolutionary war, many of these Scots-Irish "back-inhabitants" joined the revolutionary forces fighting the British. The alliance between the western and eastern soldiers was shaky at best, and skirmishes often broke out among revolutionary soldiers from different places and class backgrounds.

After the war ended, the settlers returned to the frontier to find that Native Americans had destroyed their homesteads. The settlers were also staring down an economic crisis: many soldiers still hadn't been paid the salaries owed them by the cash-strapped revolutionary government. Whiskey, instead, became the common currency of western Pennsylvania. When Alexander Hamilton announced that the government was going to tax this, the frontier's most lucrative asset, whiskey rebels, as they would be known, began tarring and feathering federal tax collectors.

George Washington led 13,000 US soldiers west to quell the rebellion. It was the first and only time a sitting US president led troops against his own citizens. Although sickness and snow drove Washington back east, his soldiers succeeded in putting down the rebels. The rebellion was over, but peace was uneasy at best. The fault lines ran deep. They would soon be tested again, by the civil war.

The history of this early east v west tension is essential reading for those who want to understand the roots of the anti-government and anti-elite attitudes held by many rural Americans. Their voices were written out of history because they lost, but that doesn't mean they disappeared. They resurfaced a century later, at places like the Battle of Gettysburg.

I grew up hearing family stories of the victory at Gettysburg. I was raised to believe that the civil war gave birth to America's greatest historical divide; the war not only set north against south, but also pitted rural farmers who relied on slavery as part of their business model against urban industrialists who didn't.

During my time reporting in western Pennsylvania, however, I began to see that the story was more complicated than that. Pennsylvania, like other states in the union, was divided along many lines. Waves of settlers with very different backgrounds had come to different parts of the area, bringing with them attitudes, expectations, and cultural traditions that were often in conflict. Posterity remembers Pennsylvania's men at arms as comrades fighting side by side, but the reality was less romantic; the soldiers were drawn together in an uneasy alliance based on shared territory, ambition and conceptions of economic advantage. I came to realize that even longstanding enmities were not as cut-and-dried as I had thought.

At the end of my time reporting in Amity, I took a trip to Gettysburg. I walked the mile from Leister Farm, where Meade headquartered the union army, through a wooded tangle of wild honeysuckle on Culp's Hill down to Spangler's Spring, where the ancestor of an Amity family at the center of my reporting, the Haneys, had fought on the side of the south. His name was Brooks —a boy soldier who collected water for Confederate troops. There on the knobby battlefield I considered the living and dead of our country, and the complicated, deep-running fissures that define it.

EVALUATING THE AUTHOR'S ARGUMENTS:

In this viewpoint, the author focuses on the ways early divisions in one part of the country can explain current divisions across the United States. Do you agree with her assessment of the forces behind the urban-rural divide? Why or why not?

The Great Migration Changed the Demographic Makeup of the United States

Office of the Historian, US House of Representatives

"This Great Migration led to the rapid growth of black urban communities in cities like New York, Chicago, St. Louis, and Detroit."

Following the end of slavery in the United States, African American men and women began moving to northern cities in large numbers. This shift, called the Great Migration, increased during World War I due to the increased demand for industrial workers. Seeking higher wages and more opportunities, African American families made their homes in cities across the Northeast, Midwest, and West. The 1920s saw a significant rise in African American activism and arts due to the greater opportunities and connections mass migration offered. The influx of new residents also shifted the racial demographics of cities like Chicago. The House Historian is the head of the Office of the Historian and is appointed by the House of Representatives to study and document its past.

"World War I And The Great Migration," Office of the Historian, US House of Representatives.

AS YOU READ, CONSIDER THE FOLLOWING QUESTIONS:
1. How many African Americans moved to northern cities between 1915 and 1920?
2. What created the labor shortages in the North that provided opportunities for workers from the South?
3. What political impact did this movement have on the African American community?

Throughout American history, wartime necessity has often opened new political and social avenues for marginalized groups. This was certainly the case after the United States intervened in the First World War in April 1917. By participating in the war effort, women suffrage activists made a compelling, and ultimately successful, case for voting rights: After all, how could America protect democracy abroad without extending it to half the population at home? Likewise, African Americans furthered their claim for racial equality at home by their contributions on European battlefields and on the home front filling industrial jobs.

Congress passed the Selective Service Act on May 10, 1917, which required all able-bodied men ages 21 to 31 to register for military duty.[1] On registration day, July 5, 1917, more than 700,000 black men enrolled. By war's end, nearly 2.3 million had answered the call. In less than two years, more than 4 million draftees swelled the ranks of the U.S. military. Of these, 367,000 were African Americans who were drafted principally into the U.S. Army. On the battlefield, many infantry units in the all-black 92nd U.S. Army Division distinguished themselves.[2] But the segregation they experienced in military service reflected the segregation in civilian life. African Americans were barred from the Marine Corps and the Army Air Corps, and in the U.S. Navy, they were assigned only menial jobs. African Americans had to fight to establish a black officer training program.[3]

Arguably the most profound effect of World War I on African Americans was the acceleration of the multi-decade mass movement of black, southern rural farm laborers northward and westward to cities in search of higher wages in industrial jobs and better social and political opportunities. This Great Migration led to the rapid growth of black

Pictured is an African American unit in the US Army during World War I. They are marching near Verdun, France.

urban communities in cities like New York, Chicago, St. Louis, and Detroit.[4] While relatively small groups of southern African Americans migrated after Reconstruction to border states such as Kansas and into the Appalachians, it was not until the imposition of Jim Crow segregation and disenfranchisement in the South that large numbers of black residents left their homes and families to search elsewhere for a better life. Still, in 1910, nearly 90 percent of African American lived in the South, four-fifths of them in rural areas.

Emigration from the South gained more traction with the advent of several important and largely economic developments beginning in the second decade of the 20th century.[5] In the South the depressed cotton market and a series of natural disasters reduced even the rare independent black landowner to sharecropping or tenant farming, trapping more and more people in a cycle of indebtedness. Military conscription and the slackening of European immigration caused massive labor shortages in the North, just as war production created an insatiable demand for industrial goods. Those labor shortages provided black Southerners with jobs in the steel, shipbuilding, and automotive industries as well as in ammunition and meat packing factories.

Many found the promise of economic opportunity irresistible, though this was not the only element pulling people northward. Contemplating departure from the South, Representative George White said to the *Chicago Daily Tribune*, "I cannot live in North Carolina and be a man and be treated as a man." In an interview with the *New York Times*, he encouraged southern black families to migrate west, "los[ing] themselves among the people of the country."[6] Historian Steven Hahn has suggested that a "pronounced self-consciousness" encompassed both social and political motivations for emigrating, "searches for new circumstances in life and labor, new sites of family and community building, new opportunities to escape economic dependence." Hahn explained that the movement not only created new political vistas but "also served as a large and powerful political transmission belt that moved and redeployed the experiences, expectations, institutions, and networks" forged in the black community during slavery and Reconstruction, which would fundamentally shape emerging centers of African-American culture and thought in the North.[7]

Whether their motivation was economic, political, individual, or communal, immense numbers of African Americans streamed northward. By one estimate, roughly a half-million southern blacks migrated to northern cities between 1915 and 1920, and between 750,000 and one million left the South in the 1920s. Chicago's black population soared 600 percent between 1910 and 1930. In the same 20-year period, Detroit's African-American community grew 2,000 percent—from 6,000 individuals to about 120,000.

This massive demographic shift dramatically altered African-American society, history, culture, and politics. During the 1920s it produced a revolutionary period of black artistic expression in literature, music, and thought known as the Harlem Renaissance. Among those who participated in this cultural moment in northern

Manhattan, which raised black consciousness nationally, were poet Langston Hughes, writer Zora Neale Hurston, and scholar and intellectual W. E. B. DuBois. A new sense of African-American culture emerged, stoked by such leaders as Marcus Garvey, an advocate for black separatism and repatriation to Africa. Garvey had emigrated from Jamaica to New York City in 1916 and, within a few years, founded the Universal Negro Improvement Association (UNIA), enlisting thousands of members.[8] UNIA found much support in the recently transplanted community of southern blacks, who helped establish many UNIA chapters in the South by sharing the organization's literature with their relatives back home.[9] No longer subject to ubiquitous voter suppression like they were in the South, skyrocketing black populations in northern cities created new opportunities for political activism. Slowly, African Americans won election to important political offices, including Oscar De Priest, a native Alabamian and future Member of Congress, who became a member of the Chicago city council in 1915.

Footnotes

1. See Adam P. Plant, "Selective Service Act of 1917," in *Major Acts of Congress*, vol. 3, ed. Brian K. Landsberg (New York: Macmillan Reference/Thompson Gale, 2004): 178–181; see also Robert W. Mullen, *Blacks in America's War: The Shift in Attitudes From the Revolutionary War to Vietnam* (New York: Monad Press, 1973).
2. Ibid., 366–374. Among these, the 15th New York Regiment of the 369th U.S. Infantry stood out. It was the first Allied unit to reach the German border on the Rhine River, and never yielded a trench or lost a member to capture. The French awarded the entire regiment the Croix de Guerre.
3. Franklin and Moss, *From Slavery to Freedom*: 361–362.
4. For more on black migrations in the post-Reconstruction period and the 20th century, see Nicholas Lemann's *The Promised Land: The Great Black Migration and How It Changed America* (New York: Knopf, 1991); Nell Irvin Painter, *Exodusters: Black Migrants to Kansas After Reconstruction* (Lawrence: University Press of Kansas, 1986); Douglas Flamming, *Bound for Freedom: Black Los Angeles in Jim Crow America* (Berkeley: University of California Press, 2005). For a concise essay on the historical literature on this topic, see Joe William Trotter, "Great Migration: An Interpretation," in *Africana: The Encyclopedia of the African and African American Experience*, vol. 3, ed. Kwame Appiah and Henry Louis Gates Jr. (New York: Oxford University Press, 2005): 53–60.
5. See the charts on regional black population shifts at the end of this essay. Migration was a long and vexing question in the South and among African-American communities generally. In 1822 the American Colonization Society (ACS) acquired a small

tract of land in the British colony of Sierra Leone in sub-Saharan Africa and named it "Liberia"—a settlement of people "made free." Approximately 15,000 free blacks from the United States migrated to Liberia over the next 20 years. Though the ACS initially received support from several prominent politicians, vocal objectors and an economic depression in Liberia killed the project by the 1830s. After Reconstruction, the issue of African migration was rekindled; however, many African-American leaders, among them John Langston, opposed foreign emigration. "Abuse us as you will, gentlemen," Langston told Democrats. "There is no way to get rid of us. This is our native country." *Congressional Record*, House, 51st Cong., 2nd sess. (16 January 1891): 1480–1482; see also William Cohen, *At Freedom's Edge: Black Mobility and the Southern White Quest for Racial Control, 1861–1915* (Baton Rouge: Louisiana State University Press, 1991).

6. "Sees No Hope in South," 26 August 1900, *Chicago Daily Tribune:* 7; "Southern Negro's Complaint," 26 August 1900, *New York Times*: 8. White lived in Washington and Philadelphia for the rest of his life. He was among eight black Congressmen in the 19th century who left the South after their service in Washington.

7. See Hahn's discussion in *A Nation Under Our Feet*: 465–476; quotations on pages 465, 466.

8. Edmund David Cronon, *Black Moses: The Story of Marcus Garvey and the Universal Negro Improvement Association* (Madison: University of Wisconsin Press, 1955): especially pages 204–207, 212–220.

9. Hahn, *A Nation Under Our Feet*: 470–473.

EVALUATING THE AUTHOR'S ARGUMENTS:

In this viewpoint, the author argues that the movement of African Americans facilitated by World War I was transformational for cities, culture, and history. Do you agree that World War I was a primary catalyst for those changes, or do you feel these shifts would have taken place without the migration launched by the conflict? In your answer, consider the cultural, historical, and economic factors the author discusses.

Viewpoint

3

The Urban-Rural Divide Manifests in Differences of Opinion

"Urban and rural communities are becoming increasingly different from each other politically."

Kim Parker, Juliana Menasce Horowitz, Anna Brown, Richard Fry, D'Vera Cohn, and Ruth Igielnik

The Pew Research Center conducts studies into opinions held on a variety of topics across many populations. In this excerpted viewpoint, researchers explain how the opinions held by urban and rural populations differ on subjects that have a direct bearing on political outcomes. By looking at issues like diversity, drug addiction, and trust in neighbors, researchers argue that the fundamental outlooks between these two populations is markedly different, changing the way they see the world. Kim Parker is director of social trends research at Pew Research Center, where Juliana Menasce Horowitz is associate director of research, Anna Brown is a research analyst, Richard Fry and Ruth Igielnik are senior researchers, and D'Vera Cohn is a senior editor and writer.

"What Unites and Divides Urban, Suburban and Rural Communities," by Kim Parker, Juliana Menasce Horowitz, Anna Brown, Richard Fry, D'Vera Cohn and Ruth Igielnik, Pew Research Center, Washington, D.C. (May 22, 2018). http://www.pewsocialtrends.org/2018/05/22/what-unites-and-divides-urban-sub-urban-and-rural-communities/. Used in accordance with Pew Research Center reuse Policy. http://www.pewresearch.org/terms-and-conditions/. Usage in no way implies endorsement.

AS YOU READ, CONSIDER THE FOLLOWING QUESTIONS:
1. What differences in outlook define rural communities and urban communities, according to this viewpoint?
2. Where do suburban communities fall in relation to the urban-rural divide?
3. Are demographics changing in the same way opinions are?

L arge demographic shifts are reshaping America. The country is growing in numbers, it's becoming more racially and ethnically diverse and the population is aging. But according to a new analysis by Pew Research Center, these trends are playing out differently across community types.

Urban areas are at the leading edge of racial and ethnic change, with nonwhites now a clear majority of the population in urban counties while solid majorities in suburban and rural areas are white. Urban and suburban counties are gaining population due to an influx of immigrants in both types of counties, as well as domestic migration into suburban areas. In contrast, rural counties have made only minimal gains since 2000 as the number of people leaving for urban or suburban areas has outpaced the number moving in. And while the population is graying in all three types of communities, this is happening more rapidly in the suburbs than in urban and rural counties.

At the same time, urban and rural communities are becoming increasingly different from each other politically. Adults in urban counties, long aligned with the Democratic Party, have moved even more to the left in recent years, and today twice as many urban voters identify as Democrats or lean Democratic as affiliate with the Republican Party. For their part, rural adults have moved more firmly into the Republican camp. More than half (54%) of rural voters now identify with or lean to the GOP, while 38% are Democrats or lean Democratic.

Against this backdrop, a new Pew Research Center survey finds that many urban and rural residents feel misunderstood and looked down on by Americans living in other types of communities. About two-thirds or more in urban and rural areas say people in other types

Residents of urban and rural communities have some concerns in common, while in other ways the issues facing their communities are quite distinct. Citizens across the United States express concerns during town hall meetings.

of communities don't understand the problems people face in their communities. And majorities of urban and rural residents say people who don't live in their type of community have a negative view of those who do. In contrast, most suburbanites say people who don't live in the suburbs have a positive view of those who do.

The divides that exist across urban, suburban and rural areas when it comes to views on social and political issues don't necessarily extend to how people are experiencing life in different types of communities. Rural and suburban adults are somewhat more rooted in their local areas, but substantial shares in cities, suburbs and rural areas say they have lived in their communities for more than 10 years. And about six-in-ten in each type of community say they feel at least some sense of attachment to their communities, though relatively few say they are *very* attached.

For adults who currently live in or near the place where they grew up—roughly half in rural areas and about four-in-ten in cities and suburbs—family ties stand out as the most important reason why they have never left or why they moved back after living away. And, when it comes to their interactions with neighbors, urban, suburban and rural residents are about equally likely to say they communicate with them on a regular basis.

In addition, urban and rural residents share some of the same concerns. Roughly equal shares of urban (50%) and rural (46%) residents say that drug addiction is a major problem in their local community. When it comes to the availability of jobs, rural adults are somewhat more likely to say this is a major problem where they live (42% say so), but a substantial share of urban dwellers (34%) say the same, significantly higher than the share in suburban communities (22%). Other problems—such as access to affordable housing in cities and access to public transportation in rural areas—are felt more acutely in some areas than in others.

The nationally representative survey of 6,251 adults was conducted online Feb. 26–March 11, 2018, using Pew Research Center's American Trends Panel. It explores the attitudes and experiences of Americans in urban, suburban and rural areas, including their views on key social and political issues, how they see people in other types of communities, and how they're living out their lives in their local communities. The survey sheds light on what divides and unites Americans across community types as well as on differences *within* urban, suburban and rural areas – sometimes driven by partisanship, sometimes by demographics. The study also includes a detailed analysis of demographic trends in urban, rural and suburban counties. Among the report's key findings:

There Are Significant Gaps in Measures of Economic Well-Being in Urban, Suburban and Rural Counties

In addition to the divergent demographic trends taking place in urban, suburban and rural communities, the analysis finds that rural counties lag behind their urban and suburban counterparts when it comes to some measures related to economic well-being. The average earnings per worker in urban areas were $49,515 in 2016, followed by $46,081 in the suburbs and $35,171 in rural areas, though these figures don't account for differences in living costs across county types. And while the number of employed adults ages 25 to 54 rose in urban and suburban counties since 2000, it declined in rural counties overall.

When it comes to the number of people living in poverty, however, the suburbs have seen much sharper increases since 2000 than urban or rural counties—a 51% increase, compared with 31% in cities and 23% in rural areas. Overall, the poverty rate is somewhat higher in rural (18%) and urban (17%) areas than in suburban (14%) counties.

Rural Americans, Especially Those Without a College Degree, Are Less Optimistic About Their Financial Future

Majorities of Americans in urban (68%), suburban (59%) and rural (62%) communities say they don't currently have enough income to lead the kind of life they want. But while about half of those in cities (46%) and suburbs (49%) who say this is the case believe they will have enough income in the future, rural residents are less optimistic: 63% of adults in rural areas who say they don't currently have enough income to lead the kind of life they want don't expect to in the future, while 36% think they eventually will.

The gap in financial optimism across community types is driven by a marked concern among rural residents without a bachelor's degree. In rural areas, about a third (34%) of those with some college or less education who say they don't currently have enough income to lead the kind of life they want think they will in the future; higher shares in cities (44%) and suburbs (46%) say this is the case. In contrast, similar shares of those with a bachelor's degree or more education in urban (53%), suburban (58%) and rural (53%) areas think they will eventually have enough income to lead the kind of life they want.

Across Community Types, Majorities Say Rural Areas Get Less Than Their Fair Share of Federal Dollars

About seven-in-ten rural residents (71%), and somewhat narrower majorities in suburban (61%) and urban (57%) communities, say rural areas receive less than their fair share of federal dollars. These views don't vary considerably across demographic or partisan lines.

When it comes to the amount urban areas receive from the federal government, about half of urban dwellers (49%) say cities receive less than their fair share; only about a third of those in suburbs and rural areas share this view. Across community types, Democrats are more likely than Republicans to say urban areas receive less than their fair share, while Republicans are more likely to say these types of communities receive *more* than their fair share. Similar shares of Democrats and Republicans within each community type say urban areas receive about the right amount of federal dollars.

About Seven-in-Ten Rural Residents Say the Values of Urban Dwellers Don't Align with Theirs; 53% of Urban Residents Say the Same About the Values of Those in Rural Areas

Most Americans say people who live in the same type of community as they do generally share their values, but they are less convinced that those in other types of communities do. For example, a majority of rural residents (58%) say the values of most people in urban areas are very or somewhat different from theirs.

Among urban dwellers, 53% see an urban-rural divide on values, while 46% say most people in rural areas have values that are similar to their own. About half in urban and rural areas say most people in suburbs share their values, while suburbanites are somewhat more likely to say most people in rural areas have values that are similar to their own (58%) than to say the same about those in urban areas (51%).

There's a clear political dimension to these attitudes. For example, majorities of Republicans in urban (64%) and suburban (78%) communities say most people in rural areas share their values, while about six-in-ten Democrats in these communities say the values of most rural residents are *different* from theirs.

Conversely, Democrats in suburban and rural areas are far more likely than their Republican counterparts to say most people who live in cities share their values. Even among Republicans who live in urban areas, only about half (48%) say most people who live in cities share their values.

Urban and Rural Americans Differ Sharply in Their Views of Some Key Social and Political Issues, but in Some Cases This Has More to Do with Partisanship than Geography

Americans in urban and rural communities have widely different views when it comes to social and political issues, including their assessments of President Donald Trump and opinions about race, immigration, same-sex marriage, abortion and the role of government.

In many cases, the differences between urban and rural residents can be attributed to the fact that rural areas tend to have a higher concentration of Republicans and Republican-leaning independents, while majorities in urban communities identify with or lean toward the Democratic Party. For example, while urban dwellers are far more likely than their rural counterparts to say abortion should be legal in all or most cases, that the government should do more to solve problems, and that whites benefit from advantages in society that black people do not have, these differences shrink when partisanship is taken into account. In other words, Democrats across community types share similar views on these issues, as do Republicans in urban, rural and suburban areas.

On other issues, differences across community types remain, even after controlling for partisanship. Rural Republicans are more likely than Republicans in urban areas to say the legalization of same-sex marriage is a bad thing for society, and they are also more likely to express very positive views of Trump. In turn, Democrats across community types express different views on immigration, with those in urban areas more likely than their rural counterparts to say the growing number of newcomers strengthens American society.

About Seven-in-Ten Urban Dwellers—vs. About Half in Rural Areas—Say It's Important to Them to Live in a Community That Is Racially and Ethnically Diverse

Rural residents are far more likely than their suburban and urban counterparts to say that, as far as they know, all or most of their neighbors are the same race or ethnicity as they are (69% vs. 53% and 43%, respectively). And urban residents place a much higher priority on living in a community that is racially and ethnically diverse than do those in suburban and rural areas: 70% of city dwellers say this is very or somewhat important to them, compared with a narrower majority of those in suburbs (59%) and about half in rural areas (52%).

Across community types, relatively few say all or most of their neighbors share their political views: About a quarter in urban (25%) and rural (24%) communities and 19% in the suburbs say this is the case. Perhaps not surprisingly, given the political makeup of urban and rural communities, majorities of Republicans in cities (59%) and Democrats in rural areas (57%) say only some or none of their neighbors share their political views.

Living among politically like-minded people is not a top priority for most Americans: Only one-in-ten or fewer in urban (10%), suburban (8%) and rural (6%) communities say it is very important to them personally to live in a community where most people share their political views. Still, many say this is at least somewhat important to them (46%, 43% and 38%, respectively).

Urban and Rural Residents See Drug Addiction as a Top-Tier Problem in Their Local Community

About half of urban (50%) and rural (46%) adults say drug addiction is a major problem where they live; a smaller but substantial share in the suburbs (35%) say the same about their local community.

Concerns about drug addiction vary significantly along socio-economic lines. Across community types, those without a bachelor's degree are more likely than those with more education to say drug addiction is a major problem in their local community.

Certain problems are felt more deeply in some types of communities than in others. For example, rural adults are more likely than their urban and suburban counterparts to say access to public transportation and to high-speed internet are major problems. For their part, urban dwellers express greater concern than those in suburban and rural areas about the availability of affordable housing, crime, poverty and the quality of K-12 education in public schools.

[…]

Across Community Types, Relatively Few Say They Feel Very Attached to the Community Where They Live

A majority of Americans (59%) say they feel some attachment to their local community, but only 16% say they feel very attached; 41% say they are not too or not at all attached to the community where they live. Adults in urban, suburban and rural areas report nearly identical levels of attachment to their local community.

In each of the three types of communities, those who have lived in their community for more than a decade and who have made connections with their neighbors are the most likely to feel a sense of attachment. About seven-in-ten adults who have lived in their community more than a decade (69%) say they feel very or somewhat attached to their local community, compared with 54% of those who have lived in their community six to 10 years and 44% of those who have done so less than six years. And while 77% of those who say they know all or most of their neighbors say they feel attached to their local community, a narrower majority of those who know some of their neighbors (55%) and about a third of those who don't know any of their neighbors (32%) say the same.

Smaller Shares of Adults in Rural Areas Than in Cities and Suburbs Say They'd Like to Move Away

About a third of U.S. adults (32%) say they would want to move to a different community if they could, while 37% say they would not want to move and 31% aren't sure. One-in-four rural residents say they would move if given the chance, compared with 37% of those in urban areas and 34% of suburbanites. Among adults younger than 30, however, about an equal share in urban (42%) and rural (39%) areas say they would move if they could; 48% of young adults in the suburbs say the same.

Among those who say they would want to move, many, particularly in suburban and rural areas, say they would like to stay in the same type of community. For example, about four-in-ten adults in the suburbs who would like to move (41%) say they would choose to move to another suburban community. Similarly, 40% of those in rural areas who report they would like to move say they would move to another rural community.

Among urban dwellers who say they would like to move, similar shares say they would like to stay in an urban area (28%) as say they would like to move to a rural community (30%). About four-in-ten (41%) would like to move to the suburbs.

Rural Residents Are More Likely than Those in Cities or Suburbs to Say They Know All or Most of Their Neighbors, but No More Likely to Interact with Them

Four-in-ten adults in rural communities say they know all or most of their neighbors, compared with 28% in the suburbs and 24% in urban areas. However, among those who know at least *some* of their neighbors, rural Americans are no more likely than their urban and suburban counterparts to say they interact with them on a regular basis.

About half of adults who know at least some of their neighbors in urban (53%), suburban (49%) and rural (47%) communities say they have face-to-face conversations with a neighbor at least once a week. Other forms of communication, such as exchanging emails or text messages or talking on the phone with neighbors, are less common: About one-in-five or fewer in urban, rural and suburban areas say this happens at least once a week.

Americans are generally trusting of their neighbors, but those in suburban and rural areas are more so. For example, about six-in-ten of those in the suburbs (62%) and in rural communities (61%) say they have a neighbor they would trust with a set of keys to their home, compared with about half (48%) in urban areas.

There is little variation among those living in different types of communities in the share reporting they have social support, feel optimistic about their lives or feel lonely. And the idea that life in the city feels more hectic than life in the country is not borne out by the data – only about one-in-ten urban, suburban and rural residents say they always or almost always feel they are too busy to enjoy their lives.

[...]

EVALUATING THE AUTHORS' ARGUMENTS:

The research explained in this viewpoint shows the differences in opinion and outlook that define urban, suburban, and rural spaces. Considering these differences, how do you think the urban-rural divide might manifest during elections?

Access to the Internet Plays a Role in Creating Divisions

"Americans who were otherwise less likely to use the Internet—such as those with lower levels of family income or education—faced an even larger disadvantage when living in a rural area."

Edward Carlson and Justin Goss

In the past twenty years, the internet has become an integral part of the way our world functions. But along with divisions in opinion and experience, urban and rural populations differ in how they experience the internet. According to studies discussed in this viewpoint, rural populations have a harder time getting access to the internet and more difficulty adopting technology. As a result, they are less connected in meaningful ways than their urban counterparts, with less access to resources, information, and news. Edward Carlson is a telecommunication policy analyst at the US Department of Commerce, where Justin Goss served as an intern at the time this viewpoint was published. Goss is now a research associate at the Public Policy Institute of California.

"The State of the Urban/Rural Digital Divide," by Edward Carlson and Justin Goss, National Telecommunications and Information Administration, U.S. Department of Commerce, August 10, 2016.

AS YOU READ, CONSIDER THE FOLLOWING QUESTIONS:
  1. What percentage of rural residents uses the internet regularly?
  2. What role does income play in determining access to the internet?
  3. What percentage of rural residents use email?

While 75 percent of Americans reported using the Internet in July 2015, the longstanding disparity between urban and rural users persists and has emerged in the adoption of new technologies such as the smartphone and social media, according to the latest computer and Internet use data collected for NTIA. This suggests that in spite of advances in both policy and technology, the barriers to Internet adoption existing in rural communities are complex and stubborn. In particular, Americans who were otherwise less likely to use the Internet—such as those with lower levels of family income or education—faced an even larger disadvantage when living in a rural area. Conversely, rural individuals with higher levels of education or family income did not have significantly lower adoption rates than their urban counterparts, according to the data. The data comes from NTIA's Computer and Internet Use Supplement to the Census Bureau's Current Population Survey.

View of the Rural Divide

While the digital divide appears to be closing for some demographic communities, the gap between rural and urban populations has remained remarkably consistent for at least as long as NTIA has been gathering data on Internet use. In 1998, 28 percent of Americans living in rural areas used the Internet, compared to 34 percent of those in urban areas. Even as Internet use increased dramatically overall, a rural/urban gap remained in 2015, with 69 percent of rural residents reporting using the Internet, versus 75 percent of urban residents. This data indicates a fairly constant 6-9 percentage point gap between rural and urban communities' Internet use over time.

Internet access and use varies considerably between urban and rural communities. In general, the percentage of urban residents who use the internet is about 6–9 percent higher than the rates of internet use in rural communities.

The Rural and Urban Divide Further Limits Low Probability Adopters

All persons, regardless of race or ethnicity, were less likely to use the Internet when living in rural areas, but certain groups of rural residents face a particularly large digital divide. For example, 78 percent of Whites nationally used the Internet in 2015, compared to 68 percent of African Americans and 66 percent of Hispanics. In rural areas, 70 percent of White Americans had adopted the Internet, compared to 59 percent of African Americans and 61 percent of Hispanics.

The digital divide also varied by family income. Nationally, Americans with family incomes between $75,000 and $99,999 per year adopted the Internet at an 83 percent rate, compared to 80 percent of those reporting income between $50,000 and $74,999, and 70 percent of those in the $25,000 to $49,999 range. These disparities were even higher among low-income rural residents. The biggest gap in Internet use between rural and urban Americans based on income came among those with incomes between $25,000 and $49,999; 66 percent of rural residents in that income range used the Internet, compared with 70 percent of their urban counterparts. In contrast, rural residents earning between $75,000 and $99,999 adopted the Internet at about the same rate as their urban counterparts.

People with lower levels of educational attainment were even more likely to find themselves on the wrong side of the digital divide when living in a rural area. Our analysis reveals that the digital divide was greatest between rural and urban users without a high school diploma. Only 52 percent of those who lack a high school diploma and live in a rural area reported using the Internet, compared with 59 percent of those who live in urban households with a similar level of education. The gap was a little smaller for high school graduates, where 63 percent of rural residents reported Internet use compared with 69 percent of urban residents and 67 percent of all Americans. Eighty-eight percent of Americans with a college degree used the Internet nationally, with rural and urban college graduates adopting at approximately the same rate.

Digital Divides Beyond Internet Adoption

Living in a rural area was also associated with lower levels of device use, Internet use at particular locations, and participation in online activities. Overall, we found rural users were less likely than their urban counterparts to report using a desktop (29 percent for rural users to 35 percent for urban users), a laptop (39 percent to 48 percent), a tablet (24 percent to 30 percent), or an Internet-enabled mobile phone (45 percent to 54 percent). Rural residents were also less likely to use the Internet from home (61 percent to 69 percent) and at work (22 percent to 29 percent). In terms of online services and functions, rural residents who indicated they *did* use the Internet were still less likely than urban residents to use email (86 percent to 92 percent), social media (68 percent to 71 percent), and online video or voice conferencing (28 percent to 38 percent) than Internet users in urban areas. While some of these differences may seem relatively modest, they are statistically significant. Lastly, rural individuals were more likely than their urban counterparts not to own any Internet compatible devices (33 percent to 26 percent), and were less likely to own more than one device.

Based on these results, it appears there is a continuing need to address the obstacles rural residents face in Internet use. For instance, some households may require subsidies to make the Internet more affordable, while others may need digital literacy training to make the Internet more useful to them. Even today, some remote rural communities still lack Internet access at all or the service available may be poor or prohibitively expensive.

NTIA has been working for the last eight years to bring affordable broadband to communities that lack it through our broadband grant program and its successor program, BroadbandUSA, which is providing technical assistance to communities seeking to expand broadband access and adoption. The latest data underscores that we still have more work to do to ensure Americans in all communities have access to affordable broadband and have the digital skills to help them enjoy the many benefits it provides.

EVALUATING THE AUTHORS' ARGUMENTS:

This viewpoint looks at the ways in which internet access differs between rural and urban populations. Considering the data, what impact do you think this difference has on way of life for urban and rural residents? Provide at least three examples based on the findings in this viewpoint.

Chapter 2

How Does the Urban-Rural Divide Impact the United States?

In recent years, the urban-rural divide has frequently been cited as a cause of increased political polarization in the United States.

There Are Real Differences in the Quality and Way of Life Between Urban and Rural Populations

"Among rural areas, poverty rates varied from a low in Connecticut (4.6 percent) to a high in New Mexico (21.9 percent)."

US Census Bureau

The US Census Bureau is responsible for carrying out regular surveys of American society. As such, it is positioned to understand how differences between rural and urban populations play out in everyday life. This viewpoint includes information on home value, poverty rate, median income, and other topics that speak to how people live in both urban and rural communities. It also examines differences that the level of rurality—or how much of a particular county is covered by rural land—has on communities. The US Census Bureau is a government agency that provides data on the country as a whole and on specific communities based on surveys.

"New Census Data Show Differences Between Urban and Rural Populations," U.S. Census Bureau, December 8, 2016.

AS YOU READ, CONSIDER THE FOLLOWING QUESTIONS:
  1. What percentage of the population is considered rural?
  2. What are the differences in education attainment between rural and urban populations?
  3. Do urban or rural communities have higher rates of poverty?

P eople who live in rural areas are more likely to own their own homes, live in their state of birth and have served in the military than their urban counterparts, according to the latest data from the U.S. Census Bureau's American Community Survey.

"I know, as both Secretary of Commerce and from my own private sector experience, that data is idle inventory on the shelf that has the power to create economic opportunity and change lives," said U.S. Secretary of Commerce Penny Pritzker. "The American Community Survey is the only survey that provides statistics that tell the story of every community's current socio-economic state, from big cities to small towns. This information is vital to making decisions in business and government that enhance the lives of all of our citizens."

As the nation's largest household survey, the American Community Survey is the only annual dataset that produces this range of statistics for all of the nation's 3,142 counties. For the three-fourths of all counties with populations too small to produce single-year statistics (2,323 counties), it is the only available dataset.

"Rural areas cover 97 percent of the nation's land area but contain 19.3 percent of the population (about 60 million people)," Census Bureau Director John H. Thompson said. "By combining five years of survey responses, the American Community Survey provides unequaled insight into the state of every community, whether large or small, urban or rural."

Today's release features data collected between 2011 and 2015 on more than 40 demographic, housing, social and economic topics, including commuting, educational attainment and home value. These statistics are available to explore on the Census Bureau website.

There were about 47 million adults 18 years and older living in rural areas. Most adults in both rural and urban areas owned their own homes but the percentage was higher in rural areas (81.1 percent

Urban and rural voters have distinct priorities and concerns. This becomes particularly clear during elections.

compared with 59.8 percent). Adults in rural areas were also more likely to live in single-family homes (78.3 percent compared with 64.6 percent) and live in their state of birth (65.4 percent compared with 48.3 percent). Veterans comprised 10.4 percent of the population of adults in rural areas compared with 7.8 percent of adults in urban areas.

Adults in rural areas had a median age of 51, making them older compared with adults in urban areas with a median age of 45. They had lower rates of poverty (11.7 percent compared with 14.0 percent) but were less likely to have obtained a bachelor's degree or higher (19.5 percent compared with 29.0). Rural communities had fewer adults born in other countries compared with those in urban areas (4.0 percent compared with 19.0 percent).

Additional findings showed:

- About 13.4 million children under the age of 18 lived in the rural areas of the nation.
- Children in rural areas had lower rates of poverty (18.9 percent compared with 22.3 percent) but more of them were uninsured (7.3 percent compared with 6.3 percent). A higher percentage

of own children in rural areas lived in married-couple households (76.3 percent compared with 67.4 percent). ("Own children" includes never-married biological, step and adopted children of the couple.)

• Compared with households in urban areas, rural households had lower median household income ($52,386 compared with $54,296), lower median home values ($151,300 compared with $190,900), and lower monthly housing costs for households paying a mortgage ($1,271 compared with $1,561). A higher percentage owned their housing units "free and clear," with no mortgage or loan (44.0 percent compared with 32.3 percent).

• States with the highest median household incomes in rural areas were Connecticut ($93,382) and New Jersey ($92,972) (not statistically different from each other). The state with the lowest rural median household income was Mississippi ($40,200). Among rural areas, poverty rates varied from a low in Connecticut (4.6 percent) to a high in New Mexico (21.9 percent).

Differences in the Rural Population
Based on Level of Rurality

Researchers also compared rural residents in 704 completely rural counties—those whose entire populations lived in rural areas—with their rural counterparts in counties that were mostly rural, and those that were mostly urban.

Between 2011 and 2015, about 9.0 percent of the rural population in the United States (5.3 million) lived in these completely rural counties, compared with about 41.0 percent (24.6 million) in the

1,185 mostly rural counties and about 50.0 percent (30.1 million) in the 1,253 mostly urban counties.

The American Community Survey five-year statistics show that the characteristics of rural residents differed depending on the level of rurality of their county of residence.

EVALUATING THE AUTHOR'S ARGUMENTS:

According to this viewpoint, the median age for rural populations is higher. Why do you think that is, and what do you think this means for rural communities today and in the future?

Health Care Inequality Between Urban and Rural Populations Is Life-Threatening

"Rural health disparities are deeply rooted in economic, social, racial, ethnic, geographic, and health workforce factors."

Robin Warshaw

The urban-rural divide is often understood as a division of opinion, but it is also a division in access to resources. Health care inequality is one example of this tangible urban-rural divide; while urban populations also have barriers to accessing care, rural communities have struggled with a lack of health care for generations. This has negatively impacted their health in serious ways and is putting rural communities in danger. This viewpoint also examines the health impacts specific to particular racial and ethnic groups in rural communities. Robin Warshaw is a freelance writer whose work focuses on health and social issues.

"Health Disparities Affect Millions in Rural U.S. Communities," by Robin Warshaw, Association of American Medical Colleges, October 31, 2017. Reprinted by permission.

AS YOU READ, CONSIDER THE FOLLOWING QUESTIONS:

1. What racial or ethnic group makes up the majority of rural residents?
2. What challenges do rural residents face in receiving medical care?
3. Are incidents of disease more or less common in rural areas?

Rural Americans—who make up at least 15 to 20% of the U.S. population—face inequities that result in worse health care than that of urban and suburban residents.

These rural health disparities are deeply rooted in economic, social, racial, ethnic, geographic, and health workforce factors. That complex mix limits access to care, makes finding solutions more difficult, and intensifies problems for rural communities everywhere.

"When you don't get your health care taken care of, you wind up with disease presentations that are much farther along. People with cancer show up with metastatic cancer, people with diabetes show up with end-organ damage," said Joseph Florence, MD, professor of family medicine and director of rural programs at Eastern Tennessee State University Quillen College of Medicine.

Consider one patient who came to a rural clinic affiliated with Quillen. The man had a large abscess that needed draining to help treat the infection. Although rural patients are less likely to have health insurance, he was insured. Yet, like many in rural areas, he couldn't find a plan provider within an hour or two of his home.

"We just happened to have a free clinic that night, so we took care of him there," said Florence. "But that's just a once-a-month event, to give medical students some experience, not a way to provide health care."

Challenges to Rural Health

U.S. rural communities—from Appalachia and the Deep South to the Midwest and western states to Alaska and Hawaii—share common risks for poorer health. These challenges, including few local doctors, poverty, and remote locations, contribute to lack of access to care.

Since most rural residents live farther away from hospitals than urban residents, it generally takes them longer to receive medical care, which can have deadly consequences.

Compared with urban areas, rural populations have lower median household incomes, a higher percentage of children living in poverty, fewer adults with postsecondary educations, more uninsured residents under age 65, and higher rates of mortality, according to a 2017 report by the North Carolina Rural Health Research Program (NC RHRP) at The University of North Carolina at Chapel Hill.

Rural residents who live on farms, ranches, reservations, and frontiers often must travel long distances to reach a health care provider. That means taking hours off from work for an initial appointment or follow-up, which causes many to delay or avoid care.

Greater distances also result in longer wait times for rural emergency medical services (EMS). That can endanger patients requiring EMS treatment. "If you're bleeding, in that extra 15 minutes (before help arrives), you can die," said Gary Hart, PhD, director of the Center for Rural Health, University of North Dakota School of Medicine and Health Sciences, in Grand Forks.

Physician shortages contribute to many rural health difficulties. Primary care doctors are stretched thin, and specialists, including mental health and substance abuse providers, are a rarity.

"Access to providers, even family physicians, is a problem," Hart said. "If you want to go to an OB/GYN, depending on where you live in the country, you may have to go 200 miles." In a study published in September 2017 by researchers from the University of Minnesota School of Public Health, as of 2014, 54% of rural counties did not have a hospital with obstetrics services.

According to the U.S. Department of Veterans Affairs (VA), 25% of U.S. veterans live in rural areas. Compared with 36% of urban military veterans, more than half of rural-dwelling veterans are enrolled in the VA health system, yet many live far from the nearest VA medical center.

Some medical schools are deliberately preparing students to meet the needs of rural populations. Quillen was founded to meet regional needs and looks for students who might be likely to "go back into a rural area and do primary care," Florence said. Students receive rural exposure during training, including through rural immersion experiences and learning from faculty with backgrounds in rural care. They conduct physicals for children in rural elementary schools and Head Start programs, gaining insight into differences with urban children.

Quillen's curriculum builds students' cultural sensitivity to rural patients. For example, said Florence, when a rural patient has gastro-intestinal pain, the doctor needs to ask, "Do you have well water? Is it a drilled well or a dug well (which is at greater risk of contamination)? Are you working in the fields, out where it's hot?"

"You have this textbook of medicine that you have to cover," he said, but the school presents that knowledge to reflect "taking care of patients in the context of where they're coming from, where they're living."

The Diversity of Rural America

While rural communities share common challenges, their residents may be racially and ethnically varied, with distinct health inequities. "We look at differences through rural-urban classifications, but when you layer in the issues of race and ethnicity, you find even greater disparities [within rural populations]," said Alana Knudson, PhD, codirector of the NORC Walsh Center for Rural Health Analysis at the University of Chicago.

African Americans are the largest rural minority. In the Deep South, once centered on the use of slaves in agriculture, some rural counties have large or majority African American populations. "There's not a lot of migration out of state. It takes a lot to leave a place you've grown up in," said Monica L. Baskin, PhD, a professor in the Division of Preventive Medicine at The University of Alabama at Birmingham (UAB) School of Medicine.

Rural African Americans have higher rates of cancer morbidity and mortality than other rural residents and have higher rates of comorbid conditions. "These are the same disparities you see nationally, with African Americans tending to have higher rates of these conditions," Baskin said. "But in the rural communities we work with [in Mississippi and Alabama], there's an even greater likelihood for them."

The most recent U.S. census, which measured population changes from 2000 to 2010, showed that rural diversity has been increasing. Non-Hispanic whites were about 80% of rural dwellers in 2010 but accounted for only 25% of rural population growth. Over that same decade, rural Hispanics increased about 45% to 3.8 million people, almost equal to rural African Americans. Native Americans increased by 8%. The number of Asians rose by about 37%, although remaining a small part of the total rural population.

In his Central Appalachian area, Florence said, the Hispanic community has grown considerably in the past 15 years, with a smaller Haitian population arriving more recently. Some are migrant workers, for whom health care is "pretty sporadic," he said. "When I see a migrant tomato farmer, he might have been without his blood pressure medicine for six months. Yet he continues to work every day."

The NC RHRP reports that at least 80 rural hospitals in 26 states have closed since January 2010. Many are in communities with significant black or Hispanic populations. One such Alabama hospital closed in September and was located in a county where 72% of residents are African American. The nearest hospitals are now about 50 minutes away.

To increase access to specialists, UAB connects patients with physicians through its telehealth program. Using technology eliminates what can be, for some patients, a four-hour drive to Birmingham, said Baskin. Some areas without internet or broadband coverage are reached through conference calls and DVDs.

Higher Disease Incidence, Worse Outcomes

The rural-urban health care divide manifests clearly in breakdowns of conditions and outcomes. According to the Centers for Disease Control and Prevention (CDC), rates for the five leading causes of death in the United States—heart disease, cancer, unintentional injury (including vehicle accidents and opioid overdoses), chronic lower respiratory disease, and stroke—are higher in rural communities.

While overall mortality rates have been declining nationwide, rural areas have had a much slower decrease. They have higher infant mortality and greater rates of mental, behavioral, and developmental disorders in children. Rural youth and rural veterans have higher rates of suicide than their urban peers.

Rural residents are also more likely to have cancers related to modifiable risks, such as tobacco use, human papillomavirus (HPV), and lack of preventive colorectal and cervical cancer screenings.

UAB has a rural cancer prevention program that trains local residents and nonprofit organizations to deliver health promotion activities and evidence-based programs. "We make sure the interventions we're doing are scalable and sustainable," Baskin said.

Although smoking has greatly decreased in much of the United States, "adults in rural counties are still smoking at the same rate, or somewhat higher, than they were 10 years ago," said Knudson. Twice as many rural youth smoke as do their urban peers, so she expects the higher rural rates of tobacco-related diseases and mortality to continue.

The CDC also cites opioid overdose deaths as 45% higher in rural areas, yet urban patients have easier access to treatment facilities.

In Central Appalachia, "we're just devastated by it," said Florence. From 2008 to 2014, rural communities saw an increase of infants born with neonatal abstinence syndrome—a condition related to maternal opioid use—that was about two and one-half times higher than in urban areas.

The factors involved in rural health disparities are "not just something that our physicians can deal with," Knudson said. "We need to figure out how to use these data to target resources and interventions to make a meaningful difference in improving the health of rural America."

EVALUATING THE AUTHOR'S ARGUMENTS:

How might lack of access to health care impact rural populations? Consider the racial, economic, and historical arguments in this viewpoint for your answer. What can be done to improve access to health care in rural communities?

Rural Communities Struggle to Compete with Urban Spaces for Young Residents

"Since the mid 1990s, rural population growth has been significantly lower than urban areas. The movement of people has resulted in national economic growth, but there are consequences."

Dipak Kumar

Any community relies on young people to ensure it thrives and grows. But rural communities have struggled in the past few decades to attract young residents, and as a result they are not growing at the same rate as cities. This is for a number of reasons, including lack of economic opportunity and resources. Finding solutions to these concerns is one of the most critical issues facing rural communities. At the time of publication, Dipak Kumar was a senior in the University of Pennsylvania's Wharton School studying management and finance. His research focuses on the intersection of business, science, and government policy.

"Rural America Is Losing Young People - Consequences and Solutions," by Dipak Kumar, Management and Finance Student, Class of 2019, The Wharton School, University of Pennsylvania, March 23, 2018. Reprinted by permission.

AS YOU READ, CONSIDER THE FOLLOWING QUESTIONS:
1. What is the growth rate of rural communities and urban communities?
2. What is "brain drain," as defined in this viewpoint?
3. What are the top three reasons young people are leaving rural communities presented in this viewpoint?

Many young Americans leave home and never return. In particular, this trend can be seen in rural America. 1,350 counties "non-metro" counties have lost population since 2010.[1] Since the mid 1990s, rural population growth has been significantly lower than urban areas.[2] The movement of people has resulted in national economic growth, but there are consequences. Behind these numbers lie worrisome consequences.

Why Young People Leave

Rural areas lack academic and economic opportunity compared to metropolises. Because of this, a large portion of migrants are talented high school graduates. This cause-effect relationship, known as "brain drain," robs rural areas of intellectual capital.

Shifting industry characteristics explains a large part of migration. Farming, logging, and mining populate the rural employment sector. Unfortunately, the sector's reliance on human capital shifted to automation, outsourcing, and foreign direct investment. The industry's evolution into today's technology dominated economy left rural inhabitants jobless.

While not an ideal outcome for rural inhabitants, the transition comes with drastic productivity gains. Today's average American farmer provides food to about 155 people compared to 25.8 people in 1960. [1] The increased output per capita enables millions to work in other industries. The impact from low rural job demand is twofold. First, the industries replacing these jobs are highly specialized and required expensive human investment. Second, rural jobs' low wages and physical nature labor are unattractive. These two factors contribute to a "chicken and egg cycle." Rural inhabitants need to

Many young people in the United States move to cities for better educational and career opportunities. This has had negative consequences for rural areas.

invest in human capital, management namely education. However, they cannot afford this development with their current wages.[2]

The economic shift pushes young people to cities. According to the U.S. Department of Commerce's Bureau of 2014 Economic Analysis, "Real GDP increased in 74% of cities."[3] Domestically, 20 cities account for over 50% of the nation's output.[4] Low headcounts in rural areas and the educational requirements of the new labor market leave young adults in rural areas with few employment choices. For instance, 50% of Oregon's jobs surround its largest city, Portland.

The Negative Consequences of Rural Population Loss

Proponents argue that economic migration supports free market allocation of labor, capital, and taxes. These classical economists believe self-regulating markets creates the most value.[5] Their points are valid. The United States has experienced dramatic economic growth, in large part because of the freedom of U.S. citizens to move to locations with economic opportunity. Although beneficial overall, the free market theory consequences of this shift are important brings a host of problems.

Rural populations governments lose their local tax base. Subsequently, local governments must cut spending.[6] The budget cuts hurt infrastructure, community centers, and most importantly public schools. As the population drops, schools close and local businesses suffer.[7] The cutbacks drive more people to cities.

Low population deflates property values. Many elderly American rely on their home equity as their savings. When property values drop, they cannot afford to sell their homes to move. In effect, young people leave their counterparts behind, effectively trapping them. The median age in rural communities has been rising.[8] In Wheeler County, Oregon, the median age rose from 48 to 56 over a 13 year period. Unfortunately, elderly populations must settle for mediocre healthcare, especially as hospitals in rural America continue to shut down, the rural elderly population left in rural areas receive mediocre medical care.[9]

National economic growth does not signify a uniform distribution of improvement. Geographical inequality traps rural Americans as evidenced by job creation location, new business location, and employment rate.[10] For example, the rural poverty rate is 15.1% contrasted against 12.9% for cities.[11]

The divergent economy creates dramatic political repercussions. The rural-urban divide grows as rural Americans feel estranged from their urban counterparts. This misalignment has entrenched itself in our political environment.

Potential Solutions

There are policies that could increase rural populations and improve rural economies. These policies revolve around encouraging young people to return to rural areas. Although rural to urban migration results in an efficient economy overall, if the goal is to ensure that rural geographic areas are not left behind relative to urban areas, encouraging young people to return to them is important. Young people must be convinced to return to rural areas. Reversing migration slows population loss, generates jobs, and increases human, social, and financial capital.[12] Data shows adult in-migration partially offsetting post high school out-migration.

Because most returnees spent time in the military or college, their education, skills, and experiences alleviate the effects of brain drain. Returners can then serve on local boards, build businesses, pay taxes, and most importantly have children.

Relocation efforts require rural policy incentivizing people to relocate to rural areas meaning that State and Federal Government would have to provide rural areas with more resources. Nationally, this type of transfer of resources already occurs through wealthier states subsidizing less wealthy states through our tax system. The following policies build upon these efforts by being more targeted towards young people who are leaving rural areas and represent an additional, needed, commitment.

Many states already implement these types of targeted policies. Because many students leave home for college, Kansas began offering state income tax breaks to out of state students if they move to a rural town in Kansas after graduation.[13] Additionally, Nebraska is experimenting with enterprise zones, which encourage business development in locations characterized by declining population, high poverty rates, and unemployment.[14] The states are waiting on evidence to assess the effectiveness of these programs.

As states experiment, the Federal government works to revitalize stale rural policy that is irrelevant in modern economic times. Traditionally, rural policy fell under the jurisdiction of the USDA and Congress's agriculture committees.[15] However, these agricultural focused committees lack the necessary holistic approach. For example, new rural policy should focus on entrepreneurship. Many young graduates migrate elsewhere because of a lack of jobs using their specific skills. Entrepreneurship requires a variety of specialized skills that align with graduates.[16] In fact, rural agriculture communities already have relatively high rates of self-employment. Unfortunately, many of these entrepreneurs have few exit options. Federal policy should create a frictionless marketplace for ownership transfer from older to younger business people. A frictionless marketplace would provide exit opportunities and a foundation for young adults. Frictionless marketplaces have already succeeded at the University of Kansas where a program helps college graduates buy rural businesses.[17]

Rural leaders must better understand how to incentivize returners. Most young people who move to rural areas grew up there. They return because of family ties and the desire to raise children in a small-town environment, surrounded by family.[18] In fact, most returnees' parents still live in the family home. The migration decision to return also hinges on school quality.[19] Lastly, the access to outdoor recreation and tranquil rustic environments pulls young adults back to rural environments.[20]

Knowing these trends, local governments can allocate their limited resources more efficiently. Resources should solidify education and environmental quality. If doing so is difficult for smaller municipalities, county areas can pool resources. Rural leaders and parents can formulate a better pitch to their young emigrants. Instead of preaching not leave at all, they should encourage exploration and work on attracting them back as they settle down to start careers and raise children. It is no coincidence, that "Median net migration rates in nonmetropolitan counties are highest among adults age 30-34 and children age 5-9."[21] That age group is most influenced by the appeal of life in rural America.

Conclusion

Although the U.S. economy is growing, rural Americans are not seeing this prosperity. Losing young people depresses rural economic conditions. The mass exodus from rural America contributed to a political divide. Rural outmigration has not just affected the United States, but will grow as an underlying economic force throughout the world. According to Global Compact for Migration, as economies continue to develop, the number of people living in cities will almost double to 6.4 billion by 2050.[22] This change will have consequences that will require future government action.

If the goal is not just economic growth but economic growth that benefits all geographies, more targeted policies towards potential returnees, and a better understanding of returnee motives will help entire countries, and not just cities, thrive.

Notes

[1] http://www.farmersfeedus.org/fun-farm-facts/

[2] https://www.theatlantic.com/business/archive/2016/06/the-graying-of-rural-america/485159/

[3] https://www.bea.gov/newsreleases/regional/gdp_metro/2015/gdp_metro0915.htm

[4] https://www.bea.gov/newsreleases/regional/gdp_metro/2015/gdp_metro0915.htm

[5] https://www.oecd.org/migration/OECD%20Migration%20Policy%20Debates%20Numero%202.pdf

[6] http://www.governing.com/topics/mgmt/states-try-to-counter-rural-flight.html

[7] https://www.theatlantic.com/magazine/archive/1997/06/slow-death-in-the-great-plains/376882/

[8] https://www.theatlantic.com/business/archive/2016/06/the-graying-of-rural-america/485159/

[9] https://www.politico.com/magazine/story/2017/10/03/meadows-medicaid-rural-hospitals-pregnant-women-dying-215671

[10] https://www.axios.com/the-large-parts-of-america-left-behind-by-todays-economy-1513305693-70d3114b-c79c-403d-902c-ec5b128f793f.html

[11] https://www.nytimes.com/roomfordebate/2016/09/19/prosperity-is-up-but-not-for-rural-america

[12] https://www.ers.usda.gov/amber-waves/2015/july/why-some-return-home-to-rural-america-and-why-it-matters/"

[13] http://www.governing.com/topics/mgmt/states-try-to-counter-rural-flight.html

[14] http://www.governing.com/topics/mgmt/states-try-to-counter-rural-flight.html

[15] https://www.cfra.org/renewrural/s/federal-policy

[16] https://www.cfra.org/renewrural/s/federal-policy

[17] http://www.governing.com/topics/mgmt/states-try-to-counter-rural-flight.html

[18] https://www.ers.usda.gov/amber-waves/2015/july/why-some-return-home-to-rural-america-and-why-it-matters/"

[19] https://www.ers.usda.gov/amber-waves/2015/july/why-some-return-home-to-rural-america-and-why-it-matters/"

[20] https://www.ers.usda.gov/amber-waves/2015/july/why-some-return-home-to-rural-america-and-why-it-matters/"

[21] https://www.ers.usda.gov/amber-waves/2015/july/why-some-return-home-to-rural-america-and-why-it-matters/"

[22] https://www.iom.int/world-migration-report-2015

EVALUATING THE AUTHOR'S ARGUMENTS:

Do you think the author's suggested solutions to the issue of outmigration address the concerns outlined in the piece? Why or why not? Use specific examples from the viewpoint and provide alternatives.

The Language Used by Urban and Rural Populations Suggests Differences in Worldview

"The... images reflect disagreements, to be sure, and contextualize our inability to find common ground on such issues as climate change, guns and the social safety net."

Michael Carolan

A word cloud is a way to visualize how commonly a particular word or idea is used, and it is therefore useful in understanding its possible importance to the person or group being studied. Here, word clouds are used to visualize how rural and urban populations respond to the same questions, offering a glimpse at how these populations see and express themselves. The differences speak to the varied worldviews not just between these two populations, but also within these populations. Michael Carolan is a professor of sociology and associate dean for research and graduate affairs in the College of Liberal Arts at Colorado State University.

AS YOU READ, CONSIDER THE FOLLOWING QUESTIONS:
1. What is the most common word used by urban populations when discussing social justice?
2. What do these word clouds say about these populations, according to the author?
3. What is one of the words used the least among rural populations when discussing autonomy?

America's political divide goes by many names—rural-urban, blue-red, metro-non-metro and left-right. We are told it is bad and that it is only getting worse, thanks to phenomena like fake news, economic uncertainty and the migration of young people away from their rural homes.

And it's fairly common for one side of the divide to speak for the other, without knowledge of who the other really is or what they stand for. An example: The term that's been used to describe my state's booming economy—"Colorado's hot streak"—is in some ways the opposite of what many rural Coloradans are experiencing. But their story rarely makes the news.

Telling someone about metro versus non-metro poverty, suicide or adult mortality rates scrapes the surface of how things are felt by those living these statistics. Descriptions never seem to do justice to how these divides are experienced, which speaks to the wisdom of the writing rule, "Show, don't tell."

What is that divide, really? And how can we show it?

How to Communicate the Divide: Word Clouds

I am a professor of sociology and have been studying rural and agriculture-related issues, both in the U.S. and abroad, since the late 1990s. Prior to that, I was busying growing up in rural Iowa, in the far northeast corner of the state.

A few years ago I interviewed farmers and agriculture professionals in North Dakota and members of a very different agricultural community: an urban farm cooperative. In the case of this particular urban farm cooperative, land was placed in a trust to support urban

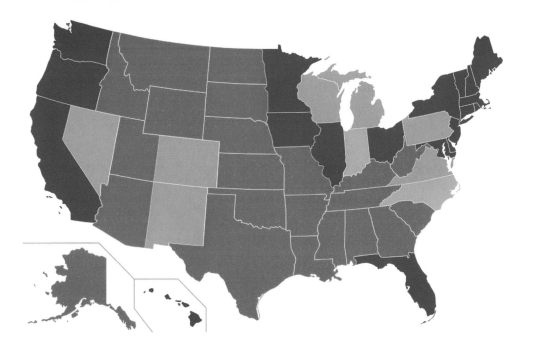

Differences in values, as demonstrated in the differences in language used by urban and rural residents, can cause states that are more urban to be politically different from those that are more rural.

agriculture and leased to members on a sliding scale. I promised not to divulge the cooperative's location in order to elicit participation within this group.

I wanted to know how these two communities talked and thought about issues like sustainability and food security. I was also interested in how these group members, whose lives were focused on agriculture in very different ways, illustrated some of the divides in our country.

I had a hunch these groups differed in more ways than their zip codes and socio-economic backgrounds. The North Dakota group, for instance, was all white and predominately male, whereas the urban population was considerably more diverse. The study eventually made its way into the peer-reviewed journal, *Rural Sociology*. As part of the study, I built four word clouds, visual representations of words I gathered from survey questions. If a picture is worth a thousand words, these particular images show more than thousands of sentences ever could: the divergent worldviews of these two groups. And they show us an angle of the aforementioned political divide that has been missed.

Individuals in each group were asked to "select three terms that describe what 'social justice' means to you" and "select three terms describing what 'autonomy' means to you."

Before giving their answer, participants were shown a list of some 50 terms, designed by me to relate specifically to each question. Other terms were explored as well, but only two terms—social justice and autonomy—are discussed here because they complement each other in interesting ways.

The terms respondents chose were then fed into software that generated word clouds, which are graphics that show the most-used terms in large letters, the least-used terms in smaller letters. (Disclaimer: I make no claims that these clouds speak for all Americans, farmers, North Dakotans, metro residents, etc. I also recognize that the cooperative experience could color the responses of those in the urban sample.)

Individual vs. Collective

Perhaps the most immediate contrast with these social justice responses lies in how the rural North Dakotans' image evokes a number of words associated with punishment, policing and due process, such

Select three terms that describe what "social justice" means to you

Urban farm cooperative

North Dakota farmers and agricultural professionals

Word clouds provided by Michael Carolan. Licensed under CC BY 4.0 International.

as "eye for an eye" and "right to attorney." These are terms associated with criminal law and the criminal justice system.

The terms chosen by the urban land cooperative, in contrast, made no reference to punishment or policing when describing their visions of social justice. Instead, they chose terms that overwhelmingly emphasized, to quote the most used term to come from this group, equity.

There was also a divergence between groups in terms of whether social justice was something individuals achieve or whether it denotes a collective response, where a community (or even society) as a whole ensures justice for individuals. To explain this point requires that I introduce two more word cloud images, produced in response to the autonomy question.

These autonomy word clouds demonstrate that the above contrasts are no fluke and are important for two reasons. First, they validate that there is something "deeper" afoot. And second, they inform the social justice images.

Note the repeated emphasis the North Dakota group placed on terms like "individualism," "self-determination," "self-rule" and "authority." In philosophical parlance, these terms align with the

Select three terms that describe what "autonomy" means to you

Urban farm cooperative

North Dakota farmers and agricultural professionals

Word clouds provided by Michael Carolan. Licensed under CC BY 4.0 International.

FAST FACT

Rural communities have a long tradition of being at the fore-front of social justice causes. For example, Harpers Ferry, West Virginia, was home to the abolitionist John Brown's 1859 raid to incite a slave revolt, and it later became the site of the first university for freed slaves.

tradition of individualism, a position that emphasizes self-reliance and that stresses human independence and liberty.

These terms also tie in well with the North Dakota group's social justice word cloud, with its emphasis on words that emphasize individual respon-sibility, e.g., "eye for an eye," and individual freedoms, "fair laws" and "right to attorney."

This stands a world away from the urban farmer cooperative group, who associated autonomy with "interdependence," "coopera-tion," "solidarity" and "community." It might appear counterintuitive to link autonomy with concepts like interdependence and solidarity, until you hear individuals from this group explain their position.

A single mother, for example, spoke directly to how indepen-dence arises for members of this group because of interdependence, rather than in spite of it.

"We can accomplish a heck of a lot more together; I feel like I have more control over my life, more independence, when we can rely on each other." She added, "I certainly appreciate how sharing childcare opportunities as a community gives me the freedom to garden. But we can't forget that farming has always been a collective effort, of sharing seed and knowledge and work."

The cooperative group's views of social justice focused significantly on community outcomes and injustices as opposed to purely individual ones. This point about the urban group expressing something resem-bling a collectivist understanding of social justice came out especially clear in the qualitative interviews with members of the cooperative.

Among the members' statements was one given by a man while he was erecting tomato cages with his two brothers, uncle and another man who 12 months prior was living in his home country of Costa Rica. Asked what social justice meant to him, he said, "Justice isn't about charity; it's about community empowerment; not about what you're given but about intentionally realizing your aspirations collectively."

Disagreements Can Lead to Dialogue

The above images reflect disagreements, to be sure, and contextualize our inability to find common ground on such issues as climate change, guns and the social safety net. If one starts from the premise that an individual can only make good, right and just decisions when they're left alone, then their position on those hot-button issues will look a lot different from those who think individual freedom is enhanced when those liberties are balanced out by constraints determined by ideas about the collective good. In short, consensus is a stretch when one "side" preaches self-reliance and self-rule while the other speaks of "independence" and needing to "rely on each other" in the same sentence, as the mother from the cooperative did.

So what does this study of these two groups and their ideas mean? Does bridging the political divide in the U.S. mean groups like this need to settle all of their political disputes and arrive at consensus about everything?

Of course not. Disagreements are good when they encourage dialogue and debate.

What we have now in our country appears to sometimes border on combativeness if not outright hate, which has me deeply concerned, both as a sociologist and a citizen.

Before we can hope to repair the divides (plural, since these differences clearly go beyond rural-urban) we need to first understand how deep they cut. You wouldn't prescribe a Band-Aid for a gash that requires stitches. The following are three concluding thoughts as we triage this wound.

Replace Caricatures with Actual Encounters

First, the opposing worldviews illustrated in the word clouds have less to do with each group having different levels of knowledge and more to do with processing knowledge through very different filters. Thus, settling political disputes by arguing over "the facts" is futile, at least in some instances.

Second, a few respondents from each group appeared to be straddling "worlds." People like this can be very helpful in bridging our political divides. Instead of building alliances based on geopolitical identities (e.g., ethnicity, political affiliation, rural/urban), we might explore how this process could start by engaging those who, like these few respondents, share similar worldviews.

Third, these worlds risk growing further apart the more their respective inhabitants look inward. The alternative would involve creating situations where we can get to know some of the people and livelihoods that are a world away from what we otherwise experience. That means the caricatures of rural and urban America need to be replaced with actual encounters.

Whoever thinks fences make for good neighbors has been infected by today's political climate. What we need are bridges. It is time we start building them—and walking across the political divide.

EVALUATING THE AUTHOR'S ARGUMENTS:

The author argues that understanding our differences can help foster dialogue. Based on these word clouds, what issues or concerns do you think would be a shared between rural and urban residents? Why do you think this?

Media Coverage Can Shape the Way We See Other People—and Ourselves

Emily Scott

"News coverage of rural America has often revolved around a set of negative narratives, including that rural areas are plagued by health problems, drug addiction, poverty, and a lack of resources and jobs."

This viewpoint examines the ways in which changing media coverage impacts the divide. In the past two decades, media coverage has shifted in ways that have changed how Americans understand their country. As correspondents gather in cities along the coasts, the middle of the country and those outside of urban spaces are often overlooked or written about in excessively simplistic terms. At the same time, the local news outlets that once reported on their communities are closing down at a rapid rate. This is influencing how Americans see rural communities and is creating division as rural communities see themselves going unrepresented. Emily Scott is a science writer at the Carl R. Woese Institute for Genomic Biology.

"Analysis: News coverage of rural America," by Emily Scott, CU-CitizenAccess.org, July 20, 2018. Reprinted by permission.

After Donald Trump won the majority of the rural vote in the 2016 presidential election, many newsrooms and media critics began to analyze how the media covers rural America.

According to a study from the Washington Post-Kaiser Family Foundation, 60 percent of rural Americans believe the media respects them "only a little" or "not at all." This comes at a time when overall trust in the media is steadily declining.

The discussion surrounding news coverage of rural America has increased as the news industry has become concentrated to the coasts and journalism jobs have become less evenly distributed throughout the country, according to a 2016 Nieman Labs report. The decline of local newspapers has been called one of the biggest crises in journalism, but some propose ways of supporting local journalism that could improve coverage.

According to 2010 data from the U.S. Census Bureau, 19.3 percent of America's population lives in rural areas—those with fewer than 2,500 people. A study from the Pew Research Center in 2012 found that people from small towns and rural areas are more likely to rely on traditional news platforms, such as TV and newspapers, whereas urban residents are more likely to consume news through "a range of digital activities," such as websites, Twitter and blogs.

Tim Marema, editor of The Daily Yonder, a multimedia news site focused on rural communities, said he believes many journalists are not aware of how rural America gets its information.

"A good piece in The New York Times is great . . . I think there's a perception that if you get that news there, everyone sees it," Marema said. "Part of the disconnect after the surprise of the election is that we didn't understand that rural America was really getting a different stream of information."

Urban-Rural Divide Growing

The 2016 presidential election showed that the urban/rural divide in America is still growing. This divide can be categorized as a political, economic, and cultural divide between urban and rural populations in the United States. A survey by the Washington Post-Kaiser Family Foundation revealed that many rural residents believe their values differ from urban residents.

Many rural Americans believe politicians and the media forget them, and this rhetoric was reinforced by Donald Trump's presidential campaign. Mike Cavender, the executive director of the Radio Television Digital News Association, said in an interview: "Trump didn't create the rural/urban divide…but he successfully exploited it and the media has been one of the primary targets of that exploitation."

For many, feeling neglected by the media and politicians has led to a sense of "rural resentment."

Katherine Cramer, a political science professor at the University of Wisconsin, described this phenomenon as the rural population feeling as if they are "not getting their fair share compared to people in the cities."

Cramer said these "intense, negative feelings against people in the cities" also have to do with struggling rural communities. Some believe opportunities and money are "going to the cities" instead of rural populations. Some have analyzed whether this phenomenon led the majority of rural residents to vote for Trump in the 2016 election.

Illinois Is One Example

The state of Illinois is one example of an urban/rural divide that has led to a stark contrast of opinions throughout the state.

An article in the Chicago Reader characterized this dynamic as "the animosity between (Chicago) and its smaller towns."

It went on to describe many Chicagoans' views of downstate Illinois as "an irrelevant agricultural appendage full of Baptists and gun owners who'd just love to turn Illinois into North Kentucky." Alternatively, downstate residents were described as being "in

According to the Pew Research Center, rural Americans tend to depend more on traditional news sources like newspapers, while urban Americans tend to get their news online.

complete opposition to the Chicago area, especially on such culturally charged matters as gun rights, LGBT rights, and abortion."

News coverage of rural America has often revolved around a set of negative narratives, including that rural areas are plagued by health problems, drug addiction, poverty, and a lack of resources and jobs.

It is true that many rural areas are struggling. A Wall Street Journal article explained some of the serious problems that rural areas are facing: aging populations, more maternity and suicide deaths, education gaps, income and net worth gaps, shrinking businesses and fewer bank loans, an increased rate of diabetes, and more. Sarah Kendzior, a St. Louis freelance writer, said the Midwest is "often ahead of the curve in terms of crises — economic, political polarization, racial strife."

Major News Outlets on Coasts

However, coverage of rural America, especially in major national news outlets, is limited because most news business is located on the coasts.

In 2014, one in five reporting jobs were located in New York City, Washington D.C., or Los Angeles. Journalism jobs are not evenly distributed throughout the country, so fewer reporters are located in areas outside these major city markets.

As media has become more digital, it has led to "greater concentration of power in the hands of a few," according to Joshua Benton, director of Nieman Journalism Lab. Additionally, local journalism has suffered as newsroom size and advertising revenue have decreased. Many counties throughout the country have no local news outlet—otherwise known as a "news desert." Many have suggested solutions to the gap in rural reporting. Heather Bryant, the director of Project Facet, proposed ideas of collaborations between newsrooms that could help support local journalism. Many of these ideas, such as joint reporting projects and embedding reporters, could be implemented between larger urban newsrooms and smaller rural newsrooms.

Tim Marema said local press in rural areas is an untapped resource for partnerships and collaborations, but he said efforts like these are difficult to ask for in the current journalism economy.

"It's hard to say 'develop better sources and get to know the issues more and spend time in places' at a period where journalists are expected to do more and more with less and less," he said.

Needs for Storytelling Networks Have Not Changed

Sam Ford, a media consultant and Knight News Innovation Fellow at Columbia University's Tow Center for Digital Journalism, has worked with rural newsrooms and studied rural communities' engagement with media.

"What was most of interest to me is that, at its core, the needs within the storytelling networks of local communities haven't changed," he said. "The way we have access to information, gathering information, (and) making sense of our communities has changed significantly in a digital age."

Ford said rural newsrooms, especially those with few staff members, could consider getting community members involved by tapping into already-established networks of communication and engagement in the community. He said rural newsrooms need sustainable resources that will enable them to gather information and understand the stories and challenges in their communities.

Journalists in small, local newsrooms can also be encouraged to stay in these newsrooms.

Kristen Hare, a reporter at the Poynter Institute, said this could be done by providing local journalists with living wages, benefits, and mentors. Hare also suggested that small newsrooms should readily accept and embrace digital changes in the industry, and that they should collaborate with larger newsrooms. Lastly, Hare said company administration needs to be transparent about layoffs and other changes to the newsroom.

If collaboration with smaller newsrooms is not possible, larger newsrooms can be educated on the issues facing rural areas and how to report on these issues, said Sarah Smarsh in a May 2018 article from Journalist's Resource, "Covering rural America: What reporters get wrong and how to get it right."

Smarsh said journalists should tap into local community resources and seek sources that can tell the community's stories. She said reporters should also avoid generalizations and stereotypes.

The issue of covering rural America adequately and accurately matters because public trust in the media is at an all-time low, according to a January 2018 report on news and public trust from the Knight Foundation. Inaccurate, inadequate reporting could lead to more distrust.

EVALUATING THE AUTHOR'S ARGUMENTS:

Based on the concerns outlined in this viewpoint, what do you feel is the most effective solution to problems regarding media representation? How do you think this solution would impact the urban-rural divide?

Chapter 3

How Can the Urban-Rural Divide Be Addressed?

While the causes of the urban-rural divide have been widely explored, finding solutions on how to bridge the divide is a challenge.

Economic Inequality Drives Tensions Between Urban and Rural Populations

Christiana K. McFarland

"Economic change and recovery in our nation have resulted in vastly different opportunities and outcomes for individuals and families based on where they live."

Rural economies have struggled in recent decades due to changes in the workforce and the increasingly globalized economy. But while urban economies have grown, experts believe that this growth could be undermined, and that strengthening rural economies can benefit the country as a whole. The relationship between rural and urban economies is far more complex than some might realize, and the prosperity of the country relies on the ties between these communities. Additionally, the data suggests that neither community should be undervalued, as both contribute about equally to states' economies. Christiana K. McFarland is the research director for the National League of Cities.

"Bridging the Urban-Rural Economic Divide," by Christiana K. McFarland, National League of Cities, 2018. Reprinted by permission.

AS YOU READ, CONSIDER THE FOLLOWING QUESTIONS:
1. Why is urban success considered vulnerable?
2. By what percentage does each $1 billion investment in rural economies create new jobs?
3. Rural communities create more of what kind of business?

The facts are stark. Economic change and recovery in our nation have resulted in vastly different opportunities and outcomes for individuals and families based on where they live. An urban-rural divide narrative is solidifying around these trends. It's one that touts (or bemoans) the all-consuming growth of our nation's largest cities and laments rural communities as devoid of economic potential. It juxtaposes urban and rural areas, pitting them against each other and, ultimately, isolating them from each other.

The narrative, whether political, economic or cultural, ignores nuances within broader urban-rural trends, all while largely avoiding solutions for more sustainable growth. Rural poverty, drug abuse, infant mortality and feelings of hopelessness are very real, but so too is rural entrepreneurship. Even, as many major cities prosper, their success has been questioned as "uniquely vulnerable to future shocks," due to gentrification, lack of affordability and industrial hyper-specialization.

It's time for the narrative to shift from urban vs. rural to a shared economic future. Bridging the economic divide between urban and rural areas will require states, regions and localities to understand and bolster *the relationship between urban and rural areas* in economically meaningful and strategic ways.

A 2011 study examining the interdependence between Minnesota's urban and rural areas found that urban regions receive substantial economic benefits from improved prosperity in rural areas. Every $1 billion increase in rural manufacturing output produces a 16% increase in urban jobs, significant additional business-to-business transactions and statewide consumer spending and investment. Similarly, a study of the Sacramento, California, region found that the majority of jobs and economic activity resulting from the region's rural food and agriculture cluster occurred in urban parts of the region. Integrated

Rural industry has a significant impact on urban areas. Studies indicate that urban communities benefit from prospering rural areas, such as those with booming agriculture and food industries.

urban and rural areas can boost each other's economies, with ripple effects of that success felt throughout the region and state.

A viable path toward long term growth, then, is to strengthen these urban-rural economic interdependencies. This approach, however, has been largely unexplored or not taken to scale with the exception of a few cases. *Bridging the Urban-Rural Economic Divide* provides a first step. This report provides an analysis of urban and rural divides in economic inputs, business environments and economic outcomes as well as the ways in which they are intertwined. These characteristics not only shape the economic landscape but over glimpses into opportunities for more impactful policies and programs to bridge the divide.

This analysis finds that:

- In all states, urban areas outpace their rural counterparts in broadband access. States with overall higher levels of broadband access also have more significant urban-rural digital divides, underscoring the importance of extending affordable broadband to rural areas.

- States with strong levels of educational attainment have less conspicuous educational divides between urban and rural areas. Often, rural areas are home to universities, which connect rural residents to educational opportunities and narrow the gap.

- Although urban areas have somewhat stronger rates of high-value business growth (growth of establishments in exporting industry sectors), rural areas don't appear disadvantaged in this characteristic. In fact, many rural areas outpace their urban counterparts in creating high-value businesses.

- Most states do not have significant urban-rural divides in prosperity growth, defined as their per capita contributions to state GDP (gross domestic product). Both urban and rural areas contribute to states' economies.

These nuanced findings show the complexities of the urban-rural divide. One consistent theme, however, is the importance of infrastructure connectivity and market access, indicating that sustainable growth hinges on the *connectedness of places*, not necessarily their designation as urban or rural.

[…]

EVALUATING THE AUTHOR'S ARGUMENTS:

This excerpted viewpoint highlights the economic differences between rural and urban spaces, but also how they are connected. How could bridging the urban-rural divide be an economic opportunity? In your answer, consider the relationships described in this viewpoint.

Viewpoint
2

Addressing Inequality Can Help Mend Divisions in Society Across Geographic Differences

"We need to dispel the myth that the goals of growing the economy and reducing inequality are necessarily in conflict, when they should actually work in concert."

Ben Olinsky

As the previous viewpoints have indicated, inequalities are at the heart of the urban-rural divide. Access to resources, care, education, and opportunity differ between regions, and addressing those differences is necessary to bridge the gap between urban and rural communities. But how can inequalities be addressed in a meaningful, effective, and economically sound way? This viewpoint lays out a few ideas that speak to the myriad issues facing communities today, including raising the minimum wage and offering more educational opportunities for people of all ages. Ben Olinksy is the senior vice president of policy and strategy at the Center for American Progress.

"6 Policies to Combat Inequality," by Ben Olinsky, Center for American Progress, January 28, 2014. Reprinted by permission.

1. What relationship exists between quality preschool education and economic growth?
2. If minimum wage increased at pace with inflation, what would it be today?
3. How much more does a former apprentice earn over their career than someone who never apprenticed?

When President Barack Obama gives his State of the Union address Tuesday, it is widely expected that he will focus on income inequality, making it a top-of-the-agenda item for this year and the remainder of his term. In his December speech hosted by the Center for American Progress, the president likely offered a preview of his message as he argued that a strong middle class helps drive economic growth:

> *We need to dispel the myth that the goals of growing the economy and reducing inequality are necessarily in conflict, when they should actually work in concert. We know from our history that our economy grows best from the middle out, when growth is more widely shared. And we know that beyond a certain level of inequality, growth actually slows altogether.*

As the consensus to build an economy that works for everyone and not just the wealthy grows, we believe that there are a few key policies that the president should call for that would begin to roll back income inequality in both the short and long term. While these policies by no means represent all that must be done to address inequality—such as protecting workers' rights on the job, improving regulation of financial markets, and limiting the corrosive influence of money in politics, to name a few—they represent new, common-sense approaches that could enjoy broad support and help restore an economy that works for everyone.

Increasing income inequality

Since 1979, states in the Northeast have recorded the largest increase in the wealth gap as fewer people control higher amounts of state income.

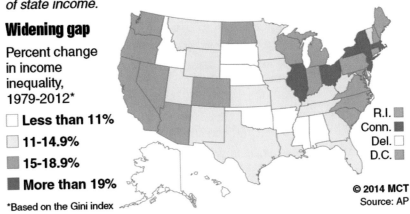

Widening gap

Percent change in income inequality, 1979-2012*

- ☐ Less than 11%
- ☐ 11-14.9%
- ▨ 15-18.9%
- ■ More than 19%

*Based on the Gini index

R.I. ▨
Conn. ■
Del. ☐
D.C. ▨

© 2014 MCT
Source: AP

Inequality is a problem for states across the country, but the wealth gap is particularly pronounced in the Northeast and West. These states tend to be more urbanized.

Raise the Minimum Wage to $10.10 per Hour

One of the most direct and efficient ways to address inequality is to raise the federal minimum wage. While average workers' wages have remained stagnant, the pay for those at the top has skyrocketed. Today, CEOs make 273 times more than average workers do—a differential that is more than 10 times larger today than it was 50 years ago. From 1968 to 2012, the American economy grew tremendously, driven in large part by a 124 percent increase in worker productivity. If the minimum wage had kept pace, it would be close to $22 per hour. Yet the minimum wage has not even kept up with inflation and is actually almost a third lower in value than it was in 1968—contributing directly to rising levels of income inequality. Raising the federal minimum wage from $7.25 to $10.10 per hour and indexing it to inflation would directly or indirectly raise the wages of 28 million workers, who would receive $35 billion in extra wages. Furthermore, polling shows that voters of both parties overwhelmingly support raising the minimum wage to $10.10.

But raising the minimum wage is not just a matter of fairness or a means of combating inequality; it is also needed to jumpstart our economy. Increasing the minimum wage would put money in the pockets of workers, who are likely to spend that money immediately at businesses in their communities. This boost in demand for goods and services will help stimulate the economy. The money then gets funneled back to employers who would need to hire more staff to keep up with the demand. Empirical research shows that raising the minimum wage, far from causing increased unemployment, will actually boost the economy and generate a virtuous cycle of increasing prosperity. If all low-wage workers earn more, virtually every American business would have more customers, and every taxpayer would have to spend less on poverty programs. Just as importantly, research shows that a higher minimum wage could positively affect economic growth by inducing more human-capital development, which can also help lower income inequality.

Increase Access to High-Quality Preschool

Low-income children are falling behind before they even step foot into kindergarten and can be months or even years behind their peers developmentally. Researchers estimate that half of the achievement gap in high school can be attributed to children's experiences before age 5. Differences between children emerge early, leading to large gaps in key skills such as vocabulary. Preschool programs can help children gain four months of additional learning, and the highest-quality programs have been shown to help children gain an additional year of learning. Children who attend high-quality preschools have positive outcomes throughout their lifetime: They are more likely to graduate from high school, attend college, and earn higher wages as adults.

In 2013, CAP proposed allowing all families to voluntarily send their children to two years of high-quality public preschool. Congress has since introduced bipartisan legislation, and 40 states already have preschool programs in their states, with conservative administrations in states such as Oklahoma and Georgia leading the way. Also last year, Republican governors in Michigan and Alabama championed new investments in preschool despite difficult fiscal constraints. In her former role as president of the U.S. Chamber of Commerce Foundation, Margaret Spellings stated that:

Business leaders strongly believe that investments in high-quality early learning for children from birth to age 5 yield high returns, not only in the lives of children but for our nation—including long-term educational, social, and economic benefits, from increased earnings and tax revenues to breaking the cycle of poverty.

Offering universal access to high-quality early education can ensure that all children, regardless of their background, start on a more level playing field, thereby combating inequality for the next generation of Americans. This approach, which has broad support, will give all children more of a fair shot to realize the American Dream by working hard and playing by the rules. It will also better prepare our workforce for the challenges of the 21st-century global economy.

Expand Apprenticeships

Apprenticeships—an "earn-while-you-learn" form of paid worker training—have been shown to significantly boost workers' lifetime wages and create pathways to well-paying careers for unemployed young workers—without incurring student debt. Many countries already rely on apprenticeships as a central tool for developing a competitive workforce, but the training model is largely unfamiliar to Americans. Apprenticeships benefit workers by connecting them with a paid job, raising their lifetime wages, and offering a postsecondary education with little or no debt. Unlike most interns, apprentices are paid employees who earn a paycheck for their work. Researchers have found that workers who complete an apprenticeship earn an average of $300,000 more in wages and benefits than comparable job seekers in their lifetime. And because they can often earn college credit for their coursework and on-the-job training, apprentices gain debt-free education at a time when the average student-loan debt for the class of 2012 is more than $29,000.

At the same time, employers who sponsor apprentices gain skilled workers, reduce employee turnover, and improve productivity. Apprenticeships can help businesses address skilled-labor shortages at a time when many employers are reporting that they cannot find skilled workers to fill jobs. In the United States, 98 percent of businesses sponsoring apprenticeships report that they would recommend them, and researchers in Canada found that Canadian employers receive a benefit of $1.47 for every $1 spent on apprenticeship training. There are a number of steps that Congress can take—and others that can be accomplished through executive action—that could help expand the use of apprenticeships in the United States.

Apprenticeships offer another option for individuals to upgrade their skills—hence their future earnings, without the need for student debt. At a time when the wage premium on postsecondary education is large, apprenticeships can be a more accessible pathway to a stronger economic future for millions of Americans and can ultimately lower levels of inequality.

Offer Universal Paid Family Leave

Income inequality directly contributes to the disparate abilities of parents to care for their children and provide them with the kind of living environment most conducive to healthy growth, success in school, and success in the workplace. Not only can wealthier parents afford high-quality child care and private pre-K, but they also disproportionately have access to flexible schedules, paid leave, and paid sick days through their employers. Their children benefit from more parental time, which translates into larger vocabularies, more attention to schooling and homework, greater attendance at parent-teacher conferences, and more and better health care.

Yet even though we know that parental time and attention is critically important for children's educational and economic outcomes, America is the only industrialized nation that does not guarantee mothers paid time off to care for a new child. Today, only 12 percent of workers have paid family leave through their employers, and low-wage workers are six times less likely to have access to paid family leave as high-income earners. In addition, women of color are disproportionately affected; they are just as likely to work as white women but are less likely to have access to benefits such as paid leave.

Offering universal paid family leave would help prevent inequality from persisting across generations. The Family and Medical Insurance Leave Act, or FAMILY Act, would provide up to 12 weeks of paid leave each year to workers for a medical condition, the birth or adoption of a new child, or the serious illness of a family member. During that time, workers could receive two-thirds of their monthly wages—up to $1,000 per week. Workers would pay into this system, with an average contribution of about $2 per week per worker from their paycheck.

Allow Americans to Refinance Their Student Debt

Student-loan debt has overtaken credit card debt and has now eclipsed $1 trillion. Yet the majority of federally backed student debt is at an interest rate higher than 6 percent. In contrast, the government can borrow money at a much lower cost, meaning that many students are paying two to three times the federal rate. Allowing students to refinance their student loans would boost the likelihood of repayment, freeing up income that could be spent in other sectors and alleviating inequality by lowering the effective cost for low-income individuals to attend college. A 2013 CAP analysis found that just refinancing federal student loans with an interest rate above 5 percent would have resulted in a savings of $14 billion for individual borrowers in 2013 and would have pumped $21 billion into the economy in the first year alone.

In recent years, college graduates' wages have been increasingly pulling away from the wages of individuals who only have a high school degree. This makes college access more critical than ever to improving economic mobility for Americans. Yet high levels of student debt can become a long-term impediment for low- and middle-income families: Graduates saddled with large monthly loan payments have to delay buying a home, are left with fewer job choices, and experience lower levels of economic stability as a result.

Improve Retirement Security

Economic inequality continues into retirement. About half of all workers do not have a retirement plan at work, and those who do have a 401(k) have only accumulated enough money to give them a monthly retirement payment of about $575 on average. Consequently, accounting firm Ernst & Young estimated that 59 percent of new middle-class retirees will outlive their savings. Furthermore, traditional defined-benefit pensions—a staple of good, middle-class jobs a generation ago—have become a rarity. The tax code also reinforces inequality in retirement; its upside-down-pyramid shape offers larger incentives for those at the top to save—even though they are already more likely to do so—and relatively little help for those at the bottom. Specifically, personal contributions to qualified retirement accounts receive a tax deduction, meaning that those in the top tax bracket, for example, receive 39.6 cents back for every dollar they save while those in the 10 percent tax bracket receive

10 cents back for every dollar they save.

However, CAP has proposed a low-cost solution that meets the needs of workers and businesses: The Secure, Accessible, Flexible, and Efficient, or SAFE, Retirement Plan would automatically enroll workers in a collective defined-contribution plan, offer low fees and professional fund management, collectively pool participants' assets, and turn these assets into lifetime payments in retirement at a low cost. Additionally, a Universal Savings Credit, which would replace all existing deductions with a new flat tax credit based on their contributions to a savings account, would flip the upside-down pyramid of tax benefits to better help low- and middle-income families save for retirement.

Conclusion

While there is no silver bullet to instantly reverse decades-long trends in rising inequality, there are common-sense policies with broad support that together can help put America back on the right path toward an economy that works for all. Adopting the six policies outlined here would go a long way to increase the wages of workers today, help all children start on a more level playing field, make skills training and postsecondary education more widely accessible, and ensure that all Americans can retire with dignity.

EVALUATING THE AUTHOR'S ARGUMENTS:

Choose two of the solutions offered in this viewpoint. How do you think they would impact rural and urban communities? Do you think this would help bridge the urban-rural divide? Why or why not?

Viewpoint

3

Longstanding Tensions Threaten the Country's Future

David Uberti

"In the early 20th century, anti-urban backlash targeted crime and unhealthy living conditions as cities ballooned into overcrowded manufacturing hubs. That sentiment took on an anti-government flavour..."

In addition to the specific inequalities and differences explored in this book, the urban-rural divide is driven in part by negative and often incorrect ideas about what people in cities and people in small towns or on farms are like. These misconceptions are damaging because they lead to policies that put communities at a disadvantage, be it farmers struggling to make ends meet or inner-city communities seeking new opportunities for growth. These misunderstandings have long been a problem for the United States, with anti-urban backlash becoming an issue in the early twentieth century. Overcoming these divisions will require addressing mistrust that has evolved over the course of decades. David Uberti is a media reporter at *VICE News* and previously reported for Gizmodo Media and the *Columbia Journalism Review*.

AS YOU READ, CONSIDER THE FOLLOWING QUESTIONS:
  1. How does the author see rural and urban communities divided politically?
  2. What was the original intent of the Electoral College?
  3. What is "white flight"?

Sitting in a downtown Cleveland coffee shop in early December, Julie Goulis is still in shock. "Some of the soul-searching I've been doing after the election has been about how I can understand people outside of my bubble," she tells me. "I was so ashamed Ohio went for Trump."

Like many US cities, Cleveland is overwhelmingly progressive in its politics and traditionally elects Democrats at all levels of government, despite hosting the 2016 Republican National Convention. But partisan divisions in the United States increasingly correlate with geographic differences, leaving many cities like Cleveland as liberal bubbles distinct from the vast conservative American hinterland. The looming inauguration of president-elect Donald Trump has left many city dwellers grappling with just how distant much of their country seems.

I meet Goulis in Tremont, a neighbourhood overlooking the Cuyahoga River as it cuts through Cleveland's revived downtown district. After an influx of European immigrants in the late 1800s, Tremont was a thriving and diverse working-class community for the first half of the 20th century, before it gradually atrophied alongside the local steel business in a familiar post-industrial spiral. Goulis, a freelance copywriter who grew up in a town about 40 miles west of Cleveland, moved here 12 years ago in search of a more walkable and diverse community. "I reject the suburbs," she says.

In the years since the housing market bottomed out, Tremont and other pockets of Cleveland have witnessed a tenuous revitalisation thanks to newcomers seeking city lifestyles and new investment in 21st-century industry. Meanwhile, other neighbourhoods, particularly communities of colour, continue to suffer from the long-term effects of deindustrialisation, disinvestment and systemic racism. The dichotomy is familiar in many American cities.

Many US cities support progressive political policies, including those in favor of open immigration laws. In general, rural communities tend to be more conservative.

Still, economically and racially diverse metropolitan areas stand as one in American politics. In Ohio, progressive urban centres like Cleveland and Columbus put up fierce opposition to Trump, who carried the state by running up huge margins in exurban and rural regions. The election only accentuated this divide in political culture, bringing a national spotlight to urban-rural tensions that have long simmered at the state level.

"I love Cleveland, but I've always considered it separate from Ohio," Goulis says. "I just feel different than my friends far out in the suburbs and the rural areas. We just have different ideas about what makes a good life."

Such conflicting perspectives stretch back to the foundation of American democracy. Urban areas—places of dense social diversity—have long been the backbone of the Democratic party, coalescing around a stronger safety net, liberal social policies, climate science and more open immigration laws. Outer suburbs and rural regions, meanwhile, are a bastion for conservative Republicans, with largely white communities rallying around traditional values, lower taxes, fewer regulations and a more static notion of American culture.

But the trends driving these divisions have quickened in recent decades, particularly during an uneven economic recovery in which many small towns were devastated and a few megacities roared back.

These kinds of demographic and economic factors that deepen the political divergence largely mirror those in liberal cities and more conservative countrysides in Europe, as the UK's Brexit vote demonstrated. In the US, the election of Trump has ushered these urban-rural divides on to the national stage like no other time in modern history.

Nowhere has the reaction been more stark than in New York, Trump's stomping ground and America's cosmopolitan flagship. Thousands of New Yorkers took to the streets in the days following his election in November, shutting down main thoroughfares as they chanted slogans like "New York hates Trump." A wall on the Union Square subway station was covered until recently with myriad neon post-it notes displaying both rants and inspiration: "No human is illegal," "Save Our Country," "The Future is Female." Occasional protests continue outside of Trump Tower in Midtown Manhattan, where the president-elect has been working to form his government.

Following a meeting there with Trump in November, Democrat New York mayor Bill de Blasio told reporters that Trump's harsh proposals on immigration "flew in the face of all that was great about New York City, the ultimate city of immigrants, the place that has succeeded because it was open for everyone." De Blasio and other urban Democrats have already pledged to remain as so-called "sanctuary cities" that provide some protections for undocumented immigrants.

The New York progressive has organised a coalition of mayors into a pro-immigration reform group called Cities for Action, and in December officials urged the Obama Administration for action before Inauguration Day. Trump, in response, has vowed to curtail federal funding to sanctuary cities, setting up another fault line should he pursue his hardline campaign promises.

This dynamic—a liberal metropolis pushing back against more conservative governments—has long played out at the state level. Politicians from New York City consistently clash with representatives from suburban Long Island or upstate New York, a largely rural region peppered with occasional post-industrial towns that tends to vote Republican. The result is a centrist state government in which de

Blasio frequently clashes with state elected officials over his avowedly liberal urban agenda.

In Ohio, where a Republican legislature has repeatedly cut taxes, reduced municipal revenue sharing, and slashed statewide services, residents in some cities have voted in favour of new local levies and additional social programmes. "From a policy perspective, we are seeing some real divergence," says Amy Hanauer, executive director of the thinktank Policy Matters Ohio.

The November presidential election saw this state-level dynamic play out on the national stage like never before. Hillary Clinton rode a wave of support in urban areas—winning 88 of the country's 100 most populous counties—en route to a popular vote lead of nearly 3 million. Perhaps more striking is that the mere 15% of counties she carried nationwide accounted for 64% of the country's aggregate GDP, according to a Brookings Institution analysis.

Trump portrayed himself as a foil to the urban liberal elite, even if the stereotype belies continued stagnation of the urban working class. He spoke of cities as dystopian hellscapes while railing against the global-facing industries that fuel their massive economic output, including finance, tech and media.

"The political divide sets up a false, zero-sum game between urban areas and rural areas, where investment and benefit for one is viewed at the expense of the other," says Alan Berube, a senior fellow at Brookings.

Anti-Urban Backlash

Americans have had such political disputes stretching back to the nation's founding. Thomas Jefferson, who envisioned the United States as an agrarian democracy, warned that, "when [people] get piled upon one another in large cities, as in Europe, they will become corrupt as in Europe." The electoral college, which allowed Trump to win the presidency despite a sizeable loss of the popular vote, was established partly to prevent populous states from gaining too much power.

In the early 20th century, anti-urban backlash targeted crime and unhealthy living conditions as cities ballooned into overcrowded manufacturing hubs. That sentiment took on an anti-government flavour following the failure of misguided urban renewal policies, and then a racist tinge once many white Americans fled to the suburbs. Urban political corruption and financial mismanagement have only deepened tensions.

"Taken together, anti-urbanism adds up to an unwillingness to acknowledge the urban and metropolitan nature of American society and the refusal to embrace the essentially collective, rather than individual, nature of urban life," writes historian Steven Conn, author of Americans Against the City: Anti-Urbanism in the Twentieth Century.

But Brookings' Berube sees cause for optimism in bridging the urban-rural divide in specific locations. "The states where there is more progress and potential," he says, "are those where the pie is growing and people see that their communities are positioned OK, and don't see themselves in a pitched battle for every last employment opportunity and investment dollar."

One example might be found in the Sun Belt, where Austin's long record of voting Democrat makes it a blue dot within Texas's sea of red. The state capital's unofficial motto, "Keep Austin Weird," was coined nearly two decades ago as an impromptu ode to local funkiness in the face of breakneck economic growth.

Since then, the university town and live music mecca has emerged as one of 21st-century America's tech centres. And its liberal social culture, which is rare in the overwhelmingly conservative Lone Star State, has remained a selling point as multinational giants such as Google set up shop, highly educated millennials flood in, and new high-rises spring up. The influx of young professionals has added a generational dimension to the differences between city and state, though it doesn't necessarily follow the usual party lines.

"That push-pull happens every legislative session, and it's something that everybody has come to expect," says Austin mayor Steve Adler, speaking generally of the Republican-controlled state government. "In those instances, Austin tries to first reinforce the liberty argument, which is to say the city government is the level of government that is closest to the people ... Our economics and our people are a little bit different – though not necessarily better— than other cities."

But the ascendent Austin, which is home to the seat of state government, may have more political clout than some of its urban counterparts across the country. In Michigan, ancestral home of the American labour movement, state Democrats have lost much of their power to dictate the state policy agenda – and it's unlikely the balance of power will shift any time soon. States draw their own federal and state political maps after each decennial census, many of them putting governing parties in control. It's no surprise, then, that new boundaries in Michigan and other states tilt the odds in the governing parties' favour.

This has come at a pivotal time for Michigan's largest city, Detroit. In 2013, residents watched as the state installed an emergency financial manager to bring the city back from the brink of financial collapse. The official guided Motown through bankruptcy, though his appointment arguably disenfranchised local voters from having a say in government.

Such moves carry an ugly connotation. In Detroit, as with so many other American cities, racism cannot be dissociated from politics and development. Black workers were barred from enjoying the full fruits of Detroit's manufacturing heyday, while black prospective homebuyers were prevented from pursuing the American dream of single family home-ownership. White flight wrought demographic devastation, with the city's population falling from about 1.9 million in 1950 to 700,000 today.

Even now, largely black residential neighbourhoods still suffer the long-term effects of this urban crisis, despite the nascent resurgence of downtown Detroit. And to Jonathan Kinloch, a businessman and activist, the election made clear that many Americans haven't even begun to grapple with that history.

"This was a test here in Michigan, in many black people's opinions, of how far we've come," Kinloch says. "The message that black people heard coming from Donald Trump, and what suburban and rural white folks heard, were two different messages. This set race relations back a long way."

A man riding a wave of implicitly anti-urban populism will now lead an increasingly urban country. His pledge to repeal Obamacare would disproportionately affect low-income and minority communities. Ben Carson, his pick to lead the Department of Housing and Urban Development, has no government or housing policy experience, once described poverty as a choice, and in 2015 compared an Obama administration fair housing rule to "mandated social-engineering schemes." And Trump's hardline stances on trade and immigration stand against the philosophical underpinnings of urban economies and culture.

The new president will assume power over diverging urban and rural Americas after accentuating the very things that separate them—a blunt departure from the once-lofty rhetoric of his predecessor. In a hyper-partisan environment in which Republicans control both houses of Congress and a vast majority of state governments, the question now is to what extent America's metropolises will wall themselves off—new city-states in a divided empire.

EVALUATING THE AUTHOR'S ARGUMENTS:

The author argues that white flight and racism played a role in establishing modern divisions between urban and rural communities. But rural areas are also diverse, and urban spaces have seen an influx of white residents due to gentrification. Do you think race continues to play a role in the urban-rural divide? If so, how?

Viewpoint 4

Immigration Could Help Rural Communities Prosper and Change the Urban-Rural Relationship

"While the stakes are high and the obstacles daunting, successfully integrating immigrants into America's rural communities can bring large dividends."

Silva Mathema, Nicole Prchal Svajlenka, and Anneliese Hermann

Immigration has long been a polarizing issue in the US and is often perceived as a dividing line between urban and rural voters. But immigrants benefit the economies they work in, and for rural communities immigrants could help counteract concerns like brain drain. Integrating immigrants into rural communities can diversify homogeneous spaces, encourage tolerance, and lead to economic growth. Silva Mathema and Nicole Prchal Svajlenka are senior policy analysts of immigrant policy at the Center for American Progress. Anneliese Hermann works for Alston and Bird, an international law firm.

"Revival and Opportunity," by Silva Mathema, Nicole Prchal Svajlenka, and Anneliese Hermann, Center for American Progress, September 2, 2018. Reprinted by permission.

AS YOU READ, CONSIDER THE FOLLOWING QUESTIONS:

1. What hurdles exist for immigrants who want to integrate into rural communities?
2. How do immigrants benefit rural economies?
3. What percentage of rural population growth is attributed to immigration?

For years, the United States has been undergoing major demographic changes that are reshaping the makeup of cities, towns, and communities all across the country. Scholars studying demographic change, particularly change tied to immigration, traditionally approach it as an urban phenomenon: first, detailing how immigrants live and work in traditional receiving communities such as New York, Los Angeles, and Boston; second, documenting how so-called new immigrant gateway cities such as Atlanta, Denver, and Charlotte, North Carolina, are experiencing rapid growth in their immigrant populations; and third, exploring the movement of immigrants to suburban areas beyond the traditional urban settings.[1] However, less research is dedicated to studying how immigrants who move to sparsely populated rural areas live in those communities and how those communities adapt to these newcomers.

According to current media coverage of rural America, the picture that emerges most often is one of economic decline, deep-rooted despair and resentment, overwhelming support for President Donald Trump and his policies that target immigrant communities. But this surface-level, one-dimensional portrayal belies a much more nuanced reality and overlooks the major positive roles immigrants are playing in rural America as well as the ways in which those significant contributions could be even more impactful.

Economic restructuring, globalization, and most recently the Great Recession have hit America's rural communities hard, and many rural areas are consistently losing more people than they are gaining through migration or birth.[2] This loss of population has brought a string of hardships to rural areas, from school and grocery store closures to the scaling back of essential health care services—including

Immigrants play a vital role in their communities, as they contribute to the workforce and create new businesses. For this reason, immigrants can help breathe new life into struggling rural communities.

hospital shutdowns. Not all rural communities are experiencing these trends equally, however. In fact, many rural communities are either experiencing a slowdown in their rate of population decline or a resurgence as immigrants and their families, as well as refugees, move into these communities in search of opportunity. In many rural communities, these new residents open small businesses, provide critically needed health care services, and supply labor for meatpacking plants, small manufacturers, dairies, fruit and vegetable farms, and other enterprises. While some rural communities adjust more easily to these demographic changes, others experience conflict, resistance, and sometimes outright anti-immigrant sentiment—adopting shortsighted policies designed to make life harder for immigrants. While the stakes are high and the obstacles daunting, successfully integrating immigrants into America's rural communities can bring large dividends.

Rural communities are a microcosm of the entire country: A number of them have had trouble adjusting to their immigrant neighbors,[3] which is reflective of a national undercurrent of anti-immigrant sentiment that has reared its ugly head of late. Understanding lessons learned from the rural experience with immigration during these polarized times is critical. This report illustrates the geography of population growth or decline in rural communities, with a particular attention to changes in the immigrant population. This analysis is followed by a discussion about what happens to communities that experience population decline and aging as well as some of the ways immigrants are helping to mitigate the negative impacts of population decline and, in some cases, putting communities on a path to prosperity. The report focuses particular attention on the economic contributions of immigrants to industries such as meatpacking, agriculture, and health care.

To a great extent, how well rural communities fare depends on how well they adjust to change and on how welcoming residents are to new immigrants.[4] This report discusses some of the strategies that several rural communities have utilized to help integrate residents and newcomers and illustrates that many constructive changes do not require significant resources.

The main findings of this report are as follows:

Immigrants Are Often Reversing or Mitigating Rural Population Decline

- Among the 2,767 rural places identified in this report, the adult population declined 4 percent—a combination of a 12 percent decline in the native-born population and a 130 percent growth among immigrants.
- Of these places, 1,894, or 68 percent, saw their population decline between 1990 and 2012–2016.
- In 78 percent of the rural places studied that experienced population decline, the decline would have been even more pronounced if not for the growth of the foreign-born population. Without immigrants, the population in these places would have contracted by 30 percent, even more staggering than the 24 percent they experienced.
- In the 873 rural places that experienced population growth, more than 1 in 5, or 21 percent, can attribute the entirety of population growth to immigrants.

Immigrants Are Leaving a Positive Mark in Rural Communities

- As immigrants and their families move to rural communities in pursuit of economic opportunity, they often bring vitality to these places.
- Immigrants provide an indispensable workforce to support communities whose local economies rely on industries such as meat processing plants, dairy farms, or fruits and vegetables farms.
- Immigrants and their families also help local economies in rural communities expand—particularly by opening grocery stores and other businesses that keep their main streets alive and thriving. Kennett Square, Pennsylvania, for example, has prospered with its large population of immigrants, who work primarily in the community's large mushroom industry and have opened bustling businesses and restaurants.[5]
- By helping to stave off population decline, a growing immigrant population in rural areas also helps keep schools open and, in some cases, even grows school enrollment.[6]
- Immigrant health care professionals such as physicians and specialists provide vital care in rural communities that are generally grappling with a shortage of doctors. In many instances, foreign-trained doctors are the only ones providing care in their area, and even then, many travel long distances to see them.[7]

Takeaways for Rural America to Integrate Their Immigrant Neighbors

Immigrant integration policies in the United States are localized, leading to divergent approaches and outcomes across communities. Some communities have proactive plans in place to integrate newcomers and allow them to capture the full set of benefits that a thriving and strong community brings. Other communities that initially struggle with their new population later implement policies that help immigrants integrate. Still, some communities have struggled to manage the demographic changes, and local politicians can sometimes worsen these situations by using negative rhetoric or even pushing for anti-immigrant policies that deepen the chasms in the community.

Communities that want to welcome immigrants, increase integration, and harness the benefits should take conscious steps to facilitate civil discussions that involve the whole community. The most critical services for immigrant families often revolve around English language learning, educational access, and social inclusion. Communities that move forward with providing these services and policies often see their immigrant populations prosper. Many of these strategies, which benefit the community as a whole, do not require significant resources to implement.

This report is the first in a series of products exploring the role of immigration in rural America. Focusing on the patterns of change, highlighting the ways in which immigrants are transforming communities, and understanding how communities deal with the challenges of rapid demographic change will not only provide the building blocks to assist rural communities and their new immigrant residents to thrive together but might also provide valuable lessons for the entire nation. In these polarized times, rural places can show the path forward on how best to overcome conflict around demographic change.

[…]

Notes

1. Audrey Singer, "The Rise of New Immigrant Gateways" (Washington: The Brookings Institution Center on Urban and Metropolitan Policy, 2004), available at https://www.brookings.edu/wp-content/uploads/2016/06/20040301_gateways.pdf; Audrey Singer, Susan W. Hardwick, and Caroline B. Brettell, *Twenty-First Century Gateways: Immigrant Incorporation in Suburban America* (Washington: Brookings Institution Press, 2008); Jill H. Wilson and Nicole Prchal Svajlenka, "Immigrants Continue to Disperse, with Fastest Growth in the Suburbs" (Washington: Brookings Institution, 2014), available at https://www.brookings.edu/research/immigrants-continue-to-disperse-with-fastest-growth-in-the-suburbs/.
2. John Cromartie, "Five Years of Population Loss in Rural and Small-Town America May Be Ending," U.S. Department of Agriculture, June 6, 2016, available at https://

www.ers.usda.gov/amber-waves/2016/june/five-years-of-population-loss-in-rural-and-small-town-america-may-be-ending/.

3. Henry Grabar, "Who Gets to Live in Fremont, Nebraska?", *Slate*, December 6, 2017, available at https://slate.com/business/2017/12/latino-immigrants-and-meatpacking-in-midwestern-towns-like-fremont-nebraska.html.

4. Ron Allen, "Immigrants impact America's heartland," NBC News, March 29, 2006, available at http://www.nbcnews.com/id/12069586/ns/nbc_nightly_news_with_brian_williams/t/immigrants-impact-americas-heartland/#.WzT3NNVKgdV.

5. Alfredo Corchado, "The Mexican Revival of Small-Town America," *The New York Times*, June 2, 2018, available at https://www.nytimes.com/2018/06/02/opinion/sunday/the-mexican-revival-of-small-town-america.html.

6. Reema Khrais and Daisy Palacios, "How Latinos are transforming the economy of a small rural town," Marketplace, September 8, 2017, available at https://www.marketplace.org/2017/09/08/business/how-latinos-transforming-economy-small-rural-town.

7. Parija Kavilanz, "Immigrant doctors in rural America are sick of waiting for green cards," CNN, June 13, 2018, available at http://money.cnn.com/2018/06/08/news/economy/immigrant-doctors-green-card-backlog/index.html.

EVALUATING THE AUTHORS' ARGUMENTS:

The authors argue that immigrants can benefit rural communities but also point out that these environments can be hostile to them. Based on this viewpoint, do you think efforts to integrate immigrants are fair to both rural communities and immigrants? Why or why not?

Viewpoint

5

The Urban-Rural Divide Is Not Going Away

Richard C. Longworth

"The same global economy that stimulates the Blue-Dot cities has ravaged the hinterlands: turning it off would not enrich the hinterlands but it would impoverish the cities."

Differences in values and economic priorities play a large role in the urban-rural divide. But while some see these as hurdles the country can move past, others aren't so sure. In this viewpoint, Richard C. Longworth argues that these differences are so fundamental that cities—or "Blue Dot America"—are effectively too deeply isolated from rural America to ever bridge the divide. As a result, cities are often left to their own devices and treated as entirely separate from the rest of the country, a phenomenon that can also be witnessed in cities around the world. Richard C. Longworth is a distinguished fellow on global cities for the Chicago Council on Global Affairs.

AS YOU READ, CONSIDER THE FOLLOWING QUESTIONS:
1. What percentage of American land is considered "Red-Tide America" by the author?
2. Urban spaces account for what percentage of the GDP?
3. How has globalization impacted rural communities?

"Blue Dot America," by Richard C. Longworth, Distinguished Fellow, The Chicago Council on Global Affairs. Reprinted by permission.

America's cities are on their own.

Post-election maps show these cities—the great global cities, state capitals, and university towns—as blue dots in a vast red sea, densely populated atolls in an otherwise scarlet tide that sweeps from coast to coast and from Canada to the Gulf.

These cities—New York and Chicago, Columbus and Atlanta, Iowa City and Ann Arbor—all voted for Hillary Clinton, often by landslide margins. The red-sea hinterland, some 97 percent of the American land mass, voted for Donald Trump, again by a landslide.

But there's more to this blue-red divide than politics. That election map is a proxy for an ever more profound split between these cities—not only Democratic but wealthier, more diverse, younger, more innovative, better-educated, more progressive, more open to the world—and their hinterlands, rebelling against a global economy that has left them behind.

This is the urban-rural split in glorious Technicolor. It is not the nation we want. But it's the nation we've got. Call it Blue-Dot America. The question now is: what do we do about it?

In the end, it comes down to values. Cities embody a set of values that clash—on election day and every day—with those of rural areas and the ruined old factory towns. Blue-Dot America faces the future; Red-Tide America embraces the past. Blue-Dot America is open to the world; Red-Tide America wants to raise the drawbridge.

Cities can sympathize with the plight of the hinterlands and the agony of good people caught in a declining economy. But it would be a tragedy if cities abandoned their values, rejected the future, slammed on the brakes, and waited for the rest of the country to catch up.

Cities are on their own in another way, too. Washington is almost literally in enemy hands, controlled by an ideology that rejects global openness, world-wide ties, immigration, trade, a rational reaction to climate change—the very life blood of cities. State governments are too often dominated by rural interests resentful of the power of cities. Cities that expect help from the traditional centers of political power will be disappointed.

If cities propose to create the future, they must do it themselves, by winning autonomy and power from the traditional centers, so they can build their own futures.

While rural areas have been hit the hardest by the decline of industry in the United States, some cities have also suffered, especially in the Rust Belt. Pictured is Cleveland, Ohio, which is one city that was negatively impacted.

Easier said than done, to say the least. The Constitution recognizes states but not cities. Legally, power flows from Washington to the state capitals, where it stops. Cities are the political vassals of the states, which have traditionally used their power to squelch any uppity city that tried to write its own rules, from gun control to immigration to minimum wages to the sugar content of soda pop.

But any city that wants to thrive in a globalizing world needs to chart its own path to answer the needs of that world, without seeking approval of backwoodsmen in the state legislatures. As David A. Graham wrote in *The Atlantic*, "the most important political and cultural divisions are not between red and blue states but between red states and the blue cities within." These divisions mark the front lines of the next big battle in American governance.

Fortunately, cities bring heavy artillery to this task. By definition, they are big, densely populated centers of civilization. Already, more than 80 percent of Americans live in metro areas: the Blue-Dot cities themselves embrace more than half the nation's population.

More important, these cities simply rule the American economy. The ten top metros account for 52 percent of the nation's gross domestic product: all are Blue-Dot cities. In 30 of the 50 states, one or two big cities account for more than half of their state's GDP. Many cities are bigger than whole nations: New York City out-produces Australia or Poland, Los Angeles out-produces the Netherlands or South Africa, Chicago out-produces Belgium or Vietnam.

Blue-Dot America has the international airports, the universities, the major media, the museums, the restaurants, the corporate headquarters, and trading floors. Theoretically, the digital revolution should scatter these assets across the landscape. In practice, it hasn't happened. Cities and their metro areas remain magnets for talent and people. They draw immigrants, because that's where the jobs are. More and more, young people are grabbing their diplomas and heading for the cities. Blue-Dot America is bleeding its red hinterlands of money and talent.

All this, of course, generalizes shamelessly. Not all Blue-Dot cities are thriving in the global economy: Detroit leads a list of cities that are both battered and shrinking. Not all city-dwellers are global citizens: the bluest of Blue-Dot cities contain a struggling middle class and vast numbers of semi-educated young people working two bad jobs to stay afloat. Millions of Blue-Dot citizens vote Republican, just as millions of Red-Tide citizens vote Democratic. Even the hard-hit, post-industrial outposts have pockets of prosperity supporting good lives.

But the dividing line, between the deepening blue and the deepening red, has become more vivid with every election. It is no generalization to say that the urban-rural split and the clash of values it describes is a reality describing two nations.

The hinterlands have real problems that cities cannot solve for them. So long as they embrace the past, they have no future.

Without question, the cities themselves have their own problems—big problems proportional to their power. Many are segregated and all are riven by class, racial and income inequalities that threaten their future. The glitter of global Chicago is tarnished by the crime and hopelessness of inter-city Chicago, barely five miles away.

But here's the point: Chicago has the means to address and even solve its problems, even its racial problems, and shame on it if it doesn't. Neither Chicago nor any other great city has the means to heal the pain of the post-industrial hinterland. The same global economy that stimulates the Blue-Dot cities has ravaged the hinterlands: turning it off would not enrich the hinterlands but it would impoverish the cities.

Which is why the cities are on their own.

But they aren't alone. Other cities, especially in Europe, face the same challenge, mostly for the same reasons. London, which lives on openness and immigration, voted to keep Britain in the European Union: the rest of England voted to pull out, a reactionary vote that literally wrapped a tourniquet around London's future. No matter how the French national election comes out this spring, Marine Le Pen's far-right National Front will get most of its votes from the nation's rural and clapped-out industrial areas, not from Paris.

Philip Stephens, a leading columnist for the *Financial Times*, even suggested that London secede from "Little England," rejoin the European Union and keep both its immigrants and Queen Elizabeth II who, after all, lives there. Stephens may have been joking a little, but not much. The leaders of American cities—Gullivers lashed down by statehouse Lilliputians—can sympathize.

The cause of the split, between city and hinterlands and between the future and the past, is no mystery. In both America and Europe, systems of governments evolved in the old industrial era, to meet the demands of that era. The great cities, embedded in their nations, powered their national economies and lived off the trade with their hinterlands.

That era is gone. It's a global era now. The economy has gone global and the global cities have led the charge, to places where national governments, by definition, cannot follow. This economy enriches the cities and impoverishes the rest. Western Europe and North America were the heart of the industrial era and the impact, for better or worse, has been most acute there.

Paris and London are as hemmed in by their national governments as American cities are by their state legislatures. Already, many of them are working together on the big issues—immigration, terrorism, climate change, inequality—through global alliances. Some of them are framing a sort of urban foreign policy, defining and promoting their global needs.

All this is new, and it's just begun.

EVALUATING THE AUTHOR'S ARGUMENTS:

In this viewpoint, the author argues that cities should become independent of rural areas. Based on the evidence in this viewpoint, do you agree with this assessment? Why or why not?

Facts About America's Urban-Rural Divide

Editor's note: These facts can be used in reports to add credibility when making important points or claims.

- Approximately 47 million adults eighteen years and older live in rural areas.
- As of 2018, 54 percent of rural voters identify with or lean to the GOP.
- Americans across the divide are concerned about drug use: 50 percent of urban residents and 46 percent of rural residents say that drug addiction is a major problem in their community.
- A lack of job prospects appears to be an issue for both communities: 42 percent of rural adults and 34 percent of urban adults say job availability is a major problem where they live.
- On average, workers in urban areas earned $49,515 per year in 2016, while rural workers earned $35,171.
- The rural poverty rate is 18 percent; the urban poverty rate is 17 percent.
- Most rural and urban residents believe rural communities are underserved, as 71 percent of rural residents and 57 percent of urban residents say rural areas receive less than their fair share of federal dollars. While 49 percent of urban residents say cities receive less than their fair share, only about 33 percent of rural residents share this view.
- Many rural residents view urban dwellers as fundamentally different from them: 58 percent of rural residents say the values of most people in urban areas are very or somewhat different from theirs. For urban residents, 53 percent see an urban-rural divide on values, while 46 percent say most people in rural areas have values that are similar to their own.
- Diversity is less common in rural communities: 69 percent of rural residents say all or most of their neighbors are the same race or ethnicity as they are. Additionally, 80 percent of rural

residents surveyed in 2010 were non-Hispanic whites.

- Political minorities feel alienated in both communities: 59 percent of Republicans in cities and 57 percent of Democrats in rural areas say only some or none of their neighbors share their political views.
- A significant percentage of Americans would move if given the chance, with 25 percent of rural residents and 37 percent of urban residents saying they would relocate if given the opportunity.
- A city has over 300,000 residents; a town has fewer than 100,000 residents.
- Close to 90 percent of African American lived in the South in 1910, mostly in rural areas. By 1920, over 1 million had migrated to northern cities.
- Internet use is similarly common in urban and rural communities, though urban dwellers have a slight advantage: 69 percent of rural residents and 75 percent of urban residents reported using the Internet in 2015.
- Veterans more commonly live in rural communities: 10.4 percent of rural residents and 7.8 percent of urban residents are veterans; 25 percent of all veterans live in rural areas.
- Urban communities are generally younger than rural ones: fifty-one years is the median adult age in rural areas; forty-five years is the median adult age in urban areas.
- A higher percentage of urban residents hold a college degree: 19.5 percent of rural residents and 29 percent of urban residents obtained bachelor's degrees.
- Immigrants make up a greater percentage of urban communities: 4 percent of rural residents and 19 percent of urban residents were born in another country.
- The median rural household income is $52,386; the median urban household income is $54,296.
- Between 2011 and 2015, 5.3 million people lived in completely rural counties, 24.6 million people lived in mostly rural counties, and 30.1 million people lived in mostly urban counties.
- Around eighty rural hospitals across twenty-six states have closed since January 2010.
- Opioid overdose death rates are 45 percent higher in rural areas.

Organizations to Contact

The editors have compiled the following list of organizations concerned with the issues debated in this book. The descriptions are derived from materials provided by the organizations. All have publications or information available for interested readers. The list was compiled on the date of publication of the present volume; the information provided here may change. Be aware that many organizations take several weeks or longer to respond to inquiries, so allow as much time as possible for the receipt of requested materials.

Center for Rural Affairs (CFRA)

145 Main Street, PO Box 136
Lyons, NE 68038
phone (402) 687-2100
email: info@cfra.org
website: www.cfra.org
CFRA is an advocacy group working to strengthen rural communities around a values-based mission. The organization works on a variety of rural and national issues.

Center for Rural Strategies

46 East Main Street
Whitesburg, KY 41858
phone: (606) 632-3244
email: teresa@ruralstrategies.org
website: www.ruralstrategies.org
The Center for Rural Strategies is a group focused on strengthening the economies and living conditions of rural communities through public information campaigns and partnerships.

The Kinder Institute for Urban Research

6100 Main Street MS-208
Houston, TX 77005-1892

phone: (713) 348-4132
email: kinder@rice.edu
website: kinder.rice.edu
Housed at Rice University, the Kinder Institute uses data and research to inform action and engagement around issues facing urban communities.

National Rural Health Association (NRHA)
4501 College Boulevard, Suite 225
Leawood, KS 66211-1921
phone: (816) 756-3140
email: mail@NRHArural.org
website: www.ruralhealthweb.org
NRHA is a research and advocacy group focused on issues related to health in rural communities, including access to care. The group works on policy and publishes reports.

Rural Policy Research Institute (RUPRI)
Institute of Public Health Research and Policy
University of Iowa College of Public Health
145 N. Riverside Drive
Iowa City, IA 52242
phone: (319) 384-3816
website: www.rupri.org
RUPRI conducts research and analysis on issues facing rural communities to inform public policy and dialogue. It is a nonpartisan group that was first organized by US senators in 1990.

Urban Institute
500 L'Enfant Plaza SW
Washington, DC 20024
phone: (202) 833-7200
website: www.urban.org
The Urban Institute is a think tank focusing on issues in urban areas, including health care, crime, housing, and development. The group hosts events and publishes reports.

For Further Reading

Books

Carr, Patrick J., and Maria J. Kefalas. *Hollowing Out the Middle*. New York, NY: Beacon Press, 2010. This book offers a consideration of brain drain in rural communities and its impact on the country.

Glaeser, Edward. *Triumph of the City*. New York, NY: Penguin Press, 2012. This title provides an examination of the growth and importance of cities.

Hoganson, Kristin L. *The Heartland*. New York, NY: Penguin Press, 2019. This book examines the history of the rural Midwest, examining globalization in the region.

Rodden, Jonathan A. *Why Cities Lose*. New York, NY: Basic Books, 2019. Readers will learn about the history of division between urban and rural communities and the impact it has on politics.

Sherman, Jennifer. *Rural Poverty in the United States*. New York, NY: Columbia University Press, 2017. This book examines the issue of poverty in rural communities throughout the US.

Speck, Jeff. *Walkable City*. New York, NY: North Point Press, 2013. This title is an examination of how cities can develop to be more walkable and the impact this would have on communities.

Woodard, Colin. *American Nations*. New York, NY: Penguin Books, 2012. The auther provides a history of regional divisions in the United States and their impact on current urban-rural divisions.

Wuthnow, Robert. *The Left Behind*. Princeton, NJ: Princeton University Press, 2019. This title offers an examination of economic decline in small-town America.

Periodicals and Internet Sources

Badger, Emily, "How the Rural-Urban Divide Became America's Political Fault Line," *New York Times,* May 21, 2019. https://www.nytimes.com/2019/05/21/upshot/america-political-divide-urban-rural.html?.

Badger, Emily, "Rural and Urban Americans, Equally Convinced the Rest of the Country Dislikes Them," *New York Times*, May 22, 2018. https://www.nytimes.com/2018/05/22/upshot/rural-and-urban-residents-feel-disparaged-pew-survey.html.

Carr, Patrick J., and Maria J. Kefalas, "The Rural Brain Drain," *The Chronicle of Higher Education*, September 21, 2009. https://www.chronicle.com/article/The-Rural-Brain-Drain/48425.

Clarke, Rory, and Claire MacDonald, "Can Healthcare Policy and Technology Heal Rural-Urban Divides?" *OECD Observer*. http://oecdobserver.org/news/fullstory.php/aid/5792/Can_healthcare_policy_and_technology_heal_rural-urban_divides_.html.

DelReal, Jose A., and Scott Clement, "New Poll of Rural Americans Shows Deep Cultural Divide with Urban Centers," *Washington Post*, June 17, 2017. https://www.chicagotribune.com/nation-world/ct-rural-americans-poll-urban-divide-20170617-story.html.

Maxwell, Rahsaan, "Why Are Urban and Rural Areas So Politically Divided?" *Washington Post*, March 5, 2019. http://www.washingtonpost.com/politics/2019/03/05/why-are-urban-rural-areas-so-politically-divided/.

Olmstead, Gracy, "The Urban-Rural Divide More Pronounced Than Ever," *American Conservative*, May 29, 2018. https://www.theamericanconservative.com/articles/the-urban-rural-divide-more-pronounced-than-ever/.

Porter, Eduardo, and Guilbert Gates, "Why Workers Without College Degrees Are Fleeing Big Cities," *New York Times*, May 21, 2019. https://www.nytimes.com/interactive/2019/05/21/business/economy/migration-big-cities.html.

Reyes, Cecilia, and Geoff Hing, "Election Analysis: On the Edge of Illinois' Urban-Rural Divide," *Chicago Tribune*, November 17, 2016. https://www.chicagotribune.com/data/ct-illinois-election-urban-rural-divide-2016-htmlstory.html.

Rubin, Jennifer, "As Small-Town America Goes, so Goes the Nation?" *Washington Post*, December 4, 2018. http://www.washingtonpost.com/opinions/2018/12/04/small-town-america-goes-so-goes-nation/.

Spectar, Jem, "Want to Close America's Rural-Urban Divide? Digital Infrastructure Is the Key." *Washington Post*, February 20,

2019. https://www.washingtonpost.com/opinions/2019/02/20/want-close-americas-rural-urban-divide-digital-infrastructure-is-key/.

Tharoor, Ishaan, "The Growing Urban-Rural Divide in Global Politics," *Washington Post,* August 9, 2018. https://www.washingtonpost.com/world/2018/08/09/growing-urban-rural-divide-global-politics/.

Van Dam, Andrew, "The Real (Surprisingly Comforting) Reason Rural America Is Doomed to Decline," *Washington Post*, May 26, 2019. https://www.washingtonpost.com/business/2019/05/24/real-surprisingly-comforting-reason-rural-america-is-doomed-decline/?utm_term=.8e50521e08a5.

Woodard, Colin, "No, the Divide in American Politics Is Not Rural vs. Urban, and Here's the Data to Prove It," *Balkanized America*, November 8, 2017. https://medium.com/s/balkanized-america/no-the-divide-in-american-politics-is-not-rural-vs-urban-and-heres-the-data-to-prove-it-c6cc8611f623.

Websites

The Daily Yonder (www.dailyyonder.com)
The Daily Yonder is a news resource published by the Center for Rural Strategies that focuses on rural issues and events. It publishes daily reporting and op-eds about issues facing rural communities.

Institute for Rural Journalism (www.ruraljournalism.org)
The Institute for Rural Journalism is a University of Kentucky institute focused on rural journalism, including developments in the field and issues facing journalists and news sources in rural communities. It publishes a daily blog of news from rural communities, as well as information on concerns about the field.

The Urban Institute (www.urban.org/features)
This website is a project by the Urban Institute that publishes interactive stories and series about issues facing urban communities. Topics include data-driven reports and stories from cities around the country.

Index

Picture Credits